Journe
Barbados,
TransAtlantic, Spa
April & May 2010

Robert (Bob) Weir stands on the safety net next to the bowsprit while sailing on the square-rig tall ship *Royal Clipper* across the Atlantic Ocean in April 2010.

Journey ...
Barbados,
TransAtlantic, Spain
April & May 2010

"Awareness of Oneness" theme, 2010

People, Places,
& Ponderings
By
Robert M (Bob) Weir

Robert M. Weir writes and speaks about people, peace, social justice, environmental issues, and outdoor adventures. Working as a freelancer, he writes contracted assignments, magazine articles, books and short stories. He is also an author's coach and edits book manuscripts for established and emerging authors. Robert's objective is to "live simply and create." He has laptop, will travel.

www.RobertMWeir.com

Press On Publishing
Kalamazoo, Michigan, USA

ISBN (assigned by Kindle Direct Publishing): 9798375123301

Also available as an eBook on Amazon.com

Dedicated to those who journey …
May you learn from others and share your knowledge wisely

Books by Robert M. Weir

Cobble Creek, short stories and poetry
Peace, Justice, Care of Earth: The Vision of John McConnell, Founder of Earth Day, biography
Dad, a diary of caring and questioning, parental care memoir
Brain Tumor: Life · Love · Lessons, medical memoir
Conversations through the Veil: Wisdom of the Spirits to Improve Our Lives, spiritual enhancement
Journey ... People, Places, & Ponderings,
    a series of 23 books on travel, adventure, and philosophy
        Michigan Adventures, 1980s to 2000s
        Great Lakes Sailing, 1990s to 2003
        A Merry Time in Maritime England, August 2001
        Barbados, TransAtlantic, Spain, April & May 2010
        Greece, Bulgaria, Historical Seas Regatta, May & June 2010
        Germany: Kassel, Berlin, Hamburg, June 2010
        Russia: St. Petersburg, Pushkin, Moscow, June 2010
        India: Delhi, The Taj Mahal, July 2010
        India: The Himalayas, July 2010
        India: Ladakh, July 2010
        India: The High Ultramarathon, July 2010
        Hawaii & The Philippines, July 2011
        India: Delhi, Ladakh & The "Road" Between, August 2011
        India: Leh, Manali, Rewalsar, August 2011
        USA: Kalachakra; India: Dalai Lama, July & September 2011
        India: Pathankot, Amritsar, Delhi, Bodh Gaya, September 2011
        India: Kolkata, 2011-2012, 2014-2015
        India: Kolkatan Candle Lighters, 2012 & 2015
        Australia: Sydney, Gold Coast, Cape Tribulation, Tasmania, Winter Holidays 2013 & 2014
        Ecuador, Switzerland, Nepal, Caribbean Cruise, 2016, 2017, 2019
        USA: Road Trips, 2011 into 2021
        USA, South: Living Legacy Pilgrimage, Civil Rights Movement, November 2016
        USA, Four Corners, Fall 2021 to Spring 2022
Reclaiming Lives: Rediscovering Myself While Educating Kolkata's Poor by Rosalie Giffoniello with Robert M Weir
MaxAbility: Who Are Your? What Are You Here For? by Jeanne Hess with Robert M Weir

Contents

Welcome

In the previous eBook, I wrote about my first significant trip out of the United States, a two-week car trip to southern England in 2001 that featured a week at the famous International Festival of the Sea and a supporting cast of stories and ruminations from Stonehenge, King Arthur's castle at Tintagel, Lands End, and others.

You can read about that part of my journey in *A Merry Time in Maritime England.*

The journey into awareness

What I thought was the trip of a lifetime
became a journey to awareness:
Awareness of our human connectivity,
our shared appetites and aspirations,
our oneness in the one Human Race,
gleaned from many people in many places.

This eBook, then, is the fourth installment in my series of travel stories titled *Journey ... People, Places, & Ponderings.* It is also the first in a subset that conveys a theme of "Awareness of Oneness," which is about my four-month journey in 2010.

There are eight eBooks in this subset. Together, they cover my three primary destinations:

- a friend's wedding in Barcelona, Spain, in May;
- the 300th birthday celebration of Pushkin, Russia, where I joined other Kalamazooans, in June; and
- a meeting with a client at an ultramarathon in the Indian Himalayas in July ...

as well as a myriad of experiences that came my way fortuitously and unexpectedly.

The stories in this eBook are about:

- my flight from my home in Kalamazoo, Michigan, to Chicago to Miami to Barbados;
- sailing on a tall ship across the Atlantic Ocean from Barbados to Azores to Spain;
- my time in Malaga and then at my friend's wedding in Barcelona.

1

The other seven eBooks in this "Awareness of Oneness" subset contain stories from:

1. *Barbados, TransAtlantic, Spain April & May 2010*, which is this eBook;
2. Greece, sailing in a tall ships regatta on the Aegean and Black seas, and then Bulgaria (*Greece, Bulgaria, Historical Seas Regatta May & June 2010*);
3. Three cities in Germany—Kassel, Berlin, and Hamburg—then sailing on a cargo vessel to St. Petersburg, Russia *(Germany: Kassel, Berlin, Hamburg June 2010);*
4. The Russian cities of St. Petersburg, Pushkin, and Moscow *(Russia: St. Petersburg, Pushkin, Moscow June 2010);*
5. Delhi and the Taj Mahal in India *(India: Delhi, The Taj Mahal July 2010);*
6. The Himalayan Mountains of India, including the infamous Leh-Manali Highway *(India: The Himalayas July 2010);*
7. The Indian state of Ladakh and the community of Leh *(India: Ladakh July 2010);*
8. An ultramarathon, The High aka La Ultra, over high Himalayan passes *(India: The High Ultramarathon July 2010).*

In the spirit of journeying as a traveler rather than a tourist, I did not depart from home with a complete itinerary. I had only my three primary destinations and partial reservations:

- my flights from Kalamazoo to Barbados;
- a Couch Surfing couch in Barbados;
- my passage on the tall ship *Royal Clipper* to Spain;
- plans to stay with my Spanish friend, the groom, in Barcelona;
- plans to stay with a client in St. Petersburg;
- provisions to meet with my Kalamazoo friends in Pushkin, Russia;
- a flight reservation from Moscow to Delhi;
- arrangements to connect with the organizer of The High in Delhi; and
- a flight reservation from Delhi to Kalamazoo, which I hurriedly changed while in Delhi.

I did not know:

- how I was going to get from Malaga to Barcelona (I researched that in Malaga);
- that I was going to be in Greece or Bulgaria nor that I would crew in the tall ships regatta (I made that arrangement while in Barcelona);
- that I would go to Germany or visit a new acquaintance who lives in Hamburg (a woman I met while crossing the Atlantic on *Royal Clipper*);
- that I would travel on a cargo ship from Lubeck, Germany, to St. Petersburg, Russia (I made that reservation while in Germany);
- that I would be met at the shipyard in St. Petersburg by a Russian sailor who I met in Varna, Bulgaria;
- that I would have a tremendously wonderful sightseeing day in Moscow with a Muscovite who I met by chance in Barcelona and who spoke excellent English; and
- how adventuresome and dangerous the journey would be to, in, and back from the Himalayas.

If I had known all that before leaving Michigan in April, the journey would not have been anywhere near as exciting as it was!

I was also determined not to pay rent while traveling. So, in early April, prior to this journey, I gave away my furniture and vacated my apartment in Kalamazoo. While this decision had been a time-consuming consternation, the freedom that I felt when I finally made the decision was tremendous. "I may no longer have a 'home,'" I told myself, "which means I can live *anywhere* now."

Ah, freedom!

My route, from left to right:
1. Flights from Kalamazoo to Barbados (red line on left);
2. voyage from Barbados to Spain (blue line on Atlantic);
3. flight from Barcelona through Germany to Greece (red line on Europe);
4. voyage in the tall ships regatta (small blue line by Turkey);
5. bus rides and flights from Bulgaria to Germany (red line in northern Europe);
6. ship from Germany to Russia (blue line at the top);
7. flight from Moscow to Delhi (long red line on right.
8. Not shown is my return flight from Delhi to Chicago nor my drive in a rental car from Chicago to Kalamazoo.

Backstory: My belief
Kalamazoo, Michigan, USA – early 2010

I believe that all people are connected; that we are all members of the Human Race, our only race; that we are all equally essential children and adults of God, connected through what *A Course in Miracles* calls the "Sonship;" that we are all eternally and infinitely loved by our Creator with whom we share and experience all creation.

I have always believed this innately, although it is only within the last three or four years that I became able to express this belief. I have always had a desire to travel, although most of my previous trips have been short and continental. So, in early 2010, I began to make plans for a journey that would take me half way around the world. The trip of a lifetime!

So while I had my three primary destinations in Spain, Russia, and India, these were simply catalysts. In truth, I set out to take the first step into the reality of my belief of human connectivity … even in faraway lands.

I traveled alone, armed only with my desire to go by water as much as possible and to avoid hotels and other aspects of tourism.

I stayed in peoples' homes. I interacted with people on streets, trains, planes, and buses. I dined with people I hadn't previously known. I engaged in international, sometimes multi-lingual conversations.

I found that where or when our ancient global connection stems from is irrelevant to me: whether from Adam being cast from a lump of clay and Eve formed from one of his ribs; or from *Australopithecus africanus* and her inquisitive, wandering descendants; or from the indigenous legends of Turtle Island and First Mother; or the Biblical Abraham and the Twelve Tribes. What matters is that we, today, recognize the beauty of being in total love with all beings and aware of our Oneness with God and with each other.

The stories that follow are my contribution to that awareness. Many other writers and photographers and humanitarians have done and are doing likewise. Together, we are adding to humanity's collective, connective consciousness. To paraphrase American cartoonist Walt Kelly and his lead character, Pogo, "We have met the others, and they are us."

This sign on the Leh-Manali Highway in India's Himalaya Mountains reflects my work ethic and purpose: to utilize my skill as a writer to connect people and instill the concept of "peace through understanding."

Robert M. Weir

Robert M (Bob) Weir

* * * * *

Erin sat at the piano
Unity Church, Kalamazoo, Michigan – February 7, 2010

Erin sat at the piano. He opened his music score and slid it an inch to the left. He wiggled on the piano stool. He adjusted his glasses. This was the time for him to do all these things, to make sure he was ready and comfortable.

In a moment, he would begin to play. Then, his hands would be busy on the keyboard, his mind would be engaged with the music. Whatever might be left undone would remain undone. And if it were major, it would affect his performance—and the audience's enjoyment.

So it is with the journey. Now is the time for me to pack and prepare, to sort and store, to sell or give away. Once on the road, the focus will be on the road. Ready or not.

An adventure with angels
Barbados and sailing across the Atlantic
article published in Encore magazine, December 2010

Wayne was a CouchSurfer host, a dark-complected man in his 60s who originated in Trinidad before moving to Canada in his 20s. He was to come to Barbados with his German girlfriend three decades ago, but when the Berlin Wall fell in 1989, she chose to reside in united Germany rather than with him in paradise.

He taught filmmaking at the University of the West Indies and produced movies but not of the Hollywood variety. "In Barbados, we make do with what we have; if we don't have it, we make it," Wayne said. He was working on a thriller, shot primarily in his two-room studio. I slept on the set amidst the sound of music from nearby bistros and chirping palm tree frogs.

Wayne took me to see three films. The first two were shorts by a Caribbean scriptwriter and producer about the influence of Indians and Africans on the islands of Trinidad and Haiti. The third was *Dead Man,* an early Johnny Depp flick, the storyline of which paled in comparison to the idyllic outdoor viewing venue: a 20-foot screen on the island's south beach, a soft breeze, lapping waves, and a dinner of tropical fish and good wine.

Having lost interest in that movie's morbid storyline, I conversed with **Lisbeth** (pronounced Lisbet), who registered guests at the cozy, two-story hotel—she called it an "apartment"—where the movie was shown. She was in her early 40s, had come from Venezuela 19 years earlier, and was still challenged by the island's numerous native and transplanted dialects. Her English was charming, with a pleasant rhythm, as we discussed physical health, spirituality, and human connectivity.

On my last morning in Barbados, I bought a coral necklace from **David**. I hadn't intended to do so, having already turned down requests by roaming beach vendors who hawked snorkeling, water skiing, and powerboat rides. But David was different. He and I met as we both, from opposite directions and with lunch in hand, approached the same makeshift bench that was nailed to a palm tree. There, gazing upon the azure sea, we sat and talked. He said I looked like a professor and asked if I worked for a local environmental organization that studied the sea and coral.

Then he showed me his necklaces, which he carried in a pouch. "My four children made them," he said. One caught my attention. Now, I'm not big on souvenirs, and I was intent on traveling light, but this one, I rationalized, weighed practically nothing, could be worn, and would not require dusting. I chose not to haggle over the price of $20 Barbadian ($10 US), in part, because David had already allowed me to take a close-up photo of his implanted tooth—gold with inset diamond—which he had found on the beach near a shipwreck.

Susie was the stewardess aboard the bus that took me from Wayne's studio to Barbados' deep water port and the tall ship that would carry me across the Atlantic. She collected my fare and placed the coins in a well-worn brown leather pouch that hung by a long strap around her neck, then, she helped me remove my 20-pound rucksack and 40-pound backpack and set them on the floor.

She was in her 40s, attractive with dark, native skin and bright eyes. Yet, her lips seldom smiled, perhaps in an attempt to hide misaligned teeth of which I caught only a glimpse. And she spoke the Queen's English. In London, she worked as a nurse. She had returned to Barbados, to her place of birth, a year earlier to care for her dying mother. With estate work nearly finished, Susie would soon depart, but her tone conveyed a desire to linger. "When you are a sensitive person, it is good to take time away; otherwise you get burned out," she said, and I had the sense she would continue to care for people no matter where she lived or worked, whether bedside or on a bus.

Mariano was among the greeting crew of the tall ship *Royal Clipper*. As a marine biologist, he would host daily lectures on aquatic life and serve on the ship's entertainment team. In the few hours prior to our departure, he helped me connect to the seaport terminal Internet network so I could send last-minute emails to a cadre of friends and clients for whom I was editing books.

We embarked that evening and, for the next 16 days, I connected with nature in the most expansive sense—far out of sight of land but afloat in a glorious vista of gently rolling ocean, sunshine, moonlight, clouds, wind that filled this magnificent vessel's five-masted rig and 42 sails, and dolphins that cavorted in our bow wake.

I also engaged in international conversation of the most stimulating nature with people from many European nations, South Africa, Great Britain, Canada, and the United States.

Royal Clipper, a luxury ship with sails, will carry 200 passengers, which she often does while cruising the Caribbean in winter and the Mediterranean in summer. But for this ocean repositioning voyage, we numbered 82 passengers and were outnumbered by crew and service staff at a ratio of two to one. Traveling alone, I enjoyed exquisite cuisine with every English-speaking person (most of them were multilingual) and others with whom I could only communicate with smiles and gestures. Topics covered the waterfront of politics, education, healthcare, history, language, customs, and culture.

People from other nations were genuinely curious about the US and knew a great deal about American history. **Bernhard** from Germany had been a young man at the end of World War II when his city, Berlin, came under control of the Allies; with his home in the American sector, he learned and could recall much about the US and its presidents. **Paul** from the Netherlands, at 24, was the youngest adult passenger; with a touch of skepticism, he asked if people in the United States care what people from other countries think. I replied with my belief that Americans who engage common folk from other lands do, but many others, those entrenched in nationalism, do not. **Robin** from the UK expressed his hope that Barack Obama be elected for a second term, and most agreed. **Jim** from Canada stated his opinion that the US "is a complicated country," which he observes with neighborly watchfulness. "Canada catches whatever the US has got," he said as though referencing the flu.

Bob came from Media, Pennsylvania, a Quaker community I know well from having lived there while researching and writing my second book, Peace, Justice, Care of Earth, in 2005. However, it quickly became apparent that he and I travel in different philosophical and political circles. Yet, for each point on which we disagreed, we found mutual respect in our shared belief that all people are a part of the one, human race.

Trevor and **Margaret** and **Stephen** and **Ann** hailed from South Africa. The latter couple owned two dairy farms and milked 1,900 head of cattle; they were concerned about a national political candidate who was telling citizens to kill farmers. The former couple had retired from a security business now owned by their son; they spoke of car thieves who use AK-47s to shoot down security helicopters. These four wanted their country to return to the ways of apartheid.

Not every conversation was deep. **Aase** from Germany taught me the fine art of signaling waiters and holding tableware and a wine glass, European style. **Joan**, who at 93 was the oldest passenger, was among the few who climbed the ratlines to enjoy an elevated view from the crow's nest. **Doris** from Germany spoke of having been married for 30 years to a man who thought a vacation was a visit to his family in Italy; since his death, she has been aboard numerous vessels, traveling more than being at home. "I started with the far-away places: Australia and New Zealand," she said.

Henning and **Gini** from Germany were aquatic consultants and marine architects who build inflatable sport boats and design diving gear. They have worked throughout the world and spoke knowledgeably of Lake Michigan and other parts of the US In regard to my journey, Henning, who wears a black patch over his right eye—"Karma in this lifetime," he said of the injury—advised: "Be a benefit to everyone not just yourself. Compare but don't criticize. Absorb but don't copy. Enjoy new places but remember your roots."

When I thanked them for speaking English, he said that English is America's gift to the world because it's easy to learn and understand. "But that's only American English," he added, "not formal British English and certainly not Texas English."

Freeform traveling (not touristing)
Spain
article published in Encore magazine, January 2011

If set properly, a single sail can pull a ship o'er the seas, but untended sails will set a vessel adrift. In Spain, Internet and credit card disconnects could have made me feel like a castaway, but two shore side people came to the rescue. One was Karim, a stranger in Malaga, and the other was Josep, a long-time friend in Barcelona.

While sailing tall ship *Royal Clipper* across the Atlantic, I was electronically out of touch for 16 days, so upon disembarking in Malaga, I wanted to contact friends and author clients for whom I was editing book manuscripts.

But, first, I needed lodging. Not having a reservation, I asked people on the streets for recommendations: some suggested the newer part of the city with its avenues and casinos, while others directed me to quaint Old Malaga.

I chose the latter and happened upon Carlos V, a hotel named after a ruler of the Holy Roman Empire and the Spanish Empire in the 1500s. Nested in the middle of a block, the establishment was a five-story structure with clean, comfortable, cozy rooms at very reasonable rates.

Not able to get online with my laptop there, I went in search of a *biblioteca* (library). Instead, at a *locaturio* (Internet café), Karim, a 24-year-old computer student from Morocco, found and fixed the problem in my Internet settings.

For the next five days, I mixed business with pleasure, working at Carlos V and taking long walks in this warm, charming Mediterranean community. Whether strolling alone or with Karim, who had offered to relate Arabian influence on Andalusian history, I found the narrow streets and wide plazas to be alive with people of all ages, day and night.

Located on the Mediterranean, Malaga is Spain's sixth most-populous city. It was founded by Phoenicians 2,700 years ago and has seen domain by Carthaginians, Romans, Arabs, and Spaniards.

Romano Teatro, a Roman theater built in the first through third centuries, was buried for nearly two millennia then rediscovered in 1951. With excavation still underway, public access was not allowed.

Looking through a chain link fence at this archeological site, we saw about 60 people, perhaps students, seated in the upper rows of the semicircular balcony. They appeared minuscule in comparison to the theater's stage and orchestra in the foreground and the adjacent edifices of Gibralfaro and Alcazaba that towered behind and above.

Alcazaba was built by the Arabs from the 8th to 11th centuries; its name means a walled fortification within a city, which aptly describes this structure of brick and stone on the lower part of Malaga's tallest hill. Gibralfaro, a castle erected by the Phoenicians in the 14th century, occupies the upper part of the same hill.

Our trek up, via a stone incline, took Karim and me more than two hours. As we climbed, we experienced ever-changing vistas of Renaissance-designed government buildings, a tree-lined boulevard, and a flower-patterned traffic circle.

Near the top, we gazed upon the harbor to the south, the Roman Catholic Catedral de Malaga and surrounding buildings to the west, and a bullring amid the city's modern hotels to the east.

At the apex, we visited a museum, roamed through gardens that included cacti and orange trees, and explored parapets that featured brick-patterned walkways and turrets with arrow loops through which we could see a valley, homes, and hills inland to the north.

We descended on a serpentine path toward a long, linear park populated with kiosks. The vendors there served food, beverages, and wares from distant lands: Egypt, Argentina, Peru, Brazil, Cuba, Galicia, Alemannia, and others.

A colorful sign extended a "welcome" in seven languages, displayed the flags of many nations, and marked this park as "Festival Intercultural." Karim explained that Malaga is a candidate in the European Capital of Culture competition.

Karim and I purchased dinner, sat on a bench under palm trees, and discussed history, religion, and philosophy as small night creatures chorused about us. Resurrecting Spanish words I had learned long ago in college, we began to speak in two languages. We parted close to midnight, but I wasn't tired and so I roamed the streets some more.

At Marques de Larios, a pedestrian mall, people strolled on a long red carpet rolled out for a film festival that had ended the day before, a Sunday. Their path was lit by ornate street lamps and lined with life-size placards of classic films.

Closer to my hotel, several eating establishments were open and serving patrons both inside and outside in this balmy clime, and street washers with a high-pressure water hose attached to a municipal truck went about their daily nocturnal chore of cleansing the city's walkways.

Malaga's streets are made of contrasting shades of marble, stone, and tile in artistic patterns of squares, diamonds, circles, and chevrons. How might they have influenced Pablo Picasso who was born in Malaga in 1881 and lived there until he was 19?

On subsequent days, I toured Museo Picasso and Catedral de Malaga. The museum features drawings of nudes, minotaurs, and bacchanalia. The magnificent stone cathedral, built in the Renaissance style between 1528 and 1782, stands nearly 100 meters tall and contains 15 chapels and 24 altars.

On my fifth and final day in Malaga, Karim took me to his mosque. It was a holy day, and the inner chamber was nearly full and reserved for Muslims. Because this zealous youth had already attempted to convert me to his faith, he was disappointed that I could not worship next to him. Nevertheless, he removed his shoes and went inside while a greeter who spoke impeccable English directed me to a courtyard within the mosque, adjacent to the inner chamber.

This area had a marble floor lined by intricately carved Arabian arches and pale sandstone walls adorned with messages from the Koran. With deference to the custom of Islam, I removed my shoes.

More men arrived, dressed in long *jellabiya,* business suits, and athletic shirts that sported the names of American teams. Kneeling and prostrating on mats, they numbered two or three hundred and prayed loudly while I, not understanding the words, sat in a corner alcove, closed my eyes, and absorbed the rhythm of their chant.

One of the prearranged parts of my trip was to attend the wedding of my friends Josep and Chus in Barcelona. I took a bus from Old Malaga to the train station where I boarded a high-speed train, part of the Spanish National Railway Network (RENFE), that left on time, traveled at 200 km/h, arrived on time, and provided complimentary ear plugs, eye shades, and bottled water for overnight travel. The next morning, Josep met me at the station and escorted me to his home.

In Barcelona, I discovered that my credit card companies had blocked my cards even though I had previously notified them I would be traveling in Europe. Using Josep's landline, I called the States and had the cards reactivated, which enabled me to make reservations for later, unplanned parts of my trip.

"Now you know the difference between a tourist and a traveler," Josep said. "A tourist goes with a plan; a traveler has only a destination from which he might not return."

Josep, an entrepreneur whose company provides turnkey computer systems for large businesses, and Chus, a teacher, live on the fifth, and top, floor of a modern condo in a high-density part of the city. They are happy people who intone the greeting, *ola,* like opening notes in a melody ... *ohhhhhh-laaaaa.*

Walking with them to market, we passed a store-front church with youth chatting outside and numerous pedestrians patronizing small, close-quartered establishments: an auto repair shop with a single garage door, *locaturios* (Internet cafés)*,* clothing and shoe stores, flower retailers, and eateries.

"It's a working man's neighborhood," Josep stated, pointing out a corner bar where, on two evenings, we joined local patrons to cheer Barcelona in national soccer championship games.

While Josep and Chus prepared for their wedding, I walked the site of the 1992 Summer Olympics, a multi-hectare campus with numerous fields and facilities where youth practiced soccer and adults played cricket.

The promenade outside the Olympic stadium contains wide terraces, curving stone stairways, and water fountains drenched in golden lamplight. There, at sunset, the wind seemed to whisper of physical prowess imbued by the world's finest athletes of nearly two decades ago.

On other days, I visited Antoni Gaudi's unfinished cathedral, walked through Poble Espanyol, an outdoor architectural museum of full-size buildings from every region in Spain, and traveled by commuter train to Montserrat, a mountain monastery outside Barcelona.

Throughout the city, people demonstrated their love of parks and efficient use of space. A car dealership on a main thoroughfare, for example, had minimized its geographic footprint by showcasing its vehicles on the first two floors of a seven-story building while the upper levels were apartment homes with balconies adorned by bicycles, plants, laundry, and sun shades.

Josep and Chus' wedding took place at city hall in a matrimonial chapel that was as ornate as any church.

At the reception, Josep's father, two of Chus' uncles, and I engaged in a challenging conversation in Catalan, Spanish, French, and English. None of us knew more than one language well, so when one spoke, others translated what few words they could. As we gained understanding, our laughter and claps on the back became idioms in the universal language of fellowship and celebration.

Barbados
Bus from airport to Oistens
Thursday, 8 April 2010, 15:30

After snaking in the customs line for an hour, I retrieve my backpack from the baggage claim, reconfigure my load, and make my way outside the Barbados airport terminal 400 meters to the bus stop.

Lumbering with a full 40-pound pack on my back and another 20-pound daypack covering my chest, I rise through the narrow door of the small shuttle bus and up three steep steps to the interior. A glance tells me that my laden body won't fit in the aisles. Nor is there a decent place to remove and set my pack in the small space behind the driver.

Before I can decide where to stand amid the dozen or so passengers who already fill the bus seats, a handsome young man in the front gets up and moves toward the middle of the bus. He stands there, holding the security bar, as I drop into the space he vacated, a single seat by the door. Then the impact hits me.

I turn toward him. He is neatly attired in a crisply ironed sky-blue dress shirt, probably a uniform that marks his position as an office or customer relations person for an airline or terminal service company. As I look at him, I am aware that I am the only pale-skinned person on the bus, a lone grain of salt in a shaker of dark pepper on an island that is almost exclusively of African descent.

Fortunately, they speak English, and I mouth, "I didn't intend to take your seat." I wonder, considering how quickly I had done exactly that, if my words come across as anything but a lie. He raises his hand in a friendly gesture and mouths, "It's okay." Still, I can't help feeling like I am the lead culprit in a throwback scene of the US South during The American Civil Rights Movement of the 1950s.

As the bus moves forward, its door still open and directing a warm, refreshing breeze flush against my face and sweaty neck, I consider the man's immediate decision, his quick action, and my instantaneous response. And the correctness of it all: This is exactly the best place for me to sit, the only place where I am not a cumbersome burden to these passengers and all who will follow and crowd the aisles, the only place where I am not a bull in a china shop of fellow humans.

How many times have I heard ministers and spiritual leaders speak of acting "for the highest good of all"? How many times have I repeated that concept to others? Now, I know the experience—thanks to this young Barbadian professional.

Making our way toward the City of Bridgetown, the dichotomy of paradise and apparent poverty is profound: The beautiful blue Caribbean is on our left, and crowded concrete-block houses with corrugated steel roofs are on our right. Voices chatter pleasantly behind me, accompanied by music from invisible speakers playing at a comfortable volume.

Then, comes a song from 1963: "He's So Fine." One of my favorite doo-lang-lang tunes from my teen years. Then comes this thought: Where am I? The female vocalist has a Caribbean accent. Definitely not The Chiffons.

I smile. I am connected. I feel at home.

Bus from Bridgetown to Holetown
Thursday, 8 April 2010, 16:20

The driver of this second bus knows two speeds: accelerate and brake.

I am still standing when the bus lurches forward. I drop into a sideways-facing seat with my packs still draping my back and chest. With my butt on the edge, I cling with my cheeks and brace my feet. Rapid acceleration slides my body toward the back of the bus. Frantic braking scoots me forward. I smile apologetically to the dark-skinned man to my right. He nods acceptance.

We are following the coastline through Bridgetown. The bus stops, named after women, are wooden canopies with a wooden bench along the sidewalk. Passengers wanting to board walk toward the curb and signal with an extended hand. Then comes the sudden braking. The door snaps open for a moment. The new arrivals drop 1.50 Barbadian dollars into the toll bin, and the coins are still clattering down the glass and metal chute when the acceleration begins again.

Soon, the bus is crowded. Young men in laborers' clothing. Women of all ages in professional dress of knee-length skirts, blouses, and jackets, some embroidered with logos of international banking institutions. The colors are centimeters from my eyes. The sleeve of a woman holding the security bar in front of me brushes my cheek. The colors are bright: red, fuchsia, orange, green, blue—the colors of Caribbean tropics and island flora, which I now glimpse out the opposite window only once in a while when a small space between the bodies in front of me appears. Those standing move toward the rear as passengers exit and replacements enter. The kaleidoscope shifts.

At one stop, a woman and a girl of about eight, wearing a white dress appropriate for a flower girl in a wedding, get off. They talk with the driver. He gives the girl a hug. She is his daughter; the woman is his wife.

The passengers are friendly people. I listen to their conversation in dialectic English that is barely understandable and I am aware that, again, I am the only paleface aboard. I ask, now and then, if Holetown is still ahead. They say it is; courteously, they promise to tell me when we are close.

Then, we are. The woman to my left asks if I know where I want to get off in Holetown. I don't. I have the address of Wayne, a CouchSurfer host who has offered a cot in his movie production studio for two nights, but I was unable to reach him by pay telephone at the airport—after discovering that my cell phone doesn't work even though it has an international SIM card.

I talk to the driver. Holetown has four stops. I choose the second.

At the bus stop, a young woman lets me use her cell phone. Wayne answers this time. I tell him where I am, and he tells me to cross the street and wait inside a mall with about a dozen shops. He arrives within ten minutes. It turns out that I am only four blocks from his studio. Somehow, I made the right choice.

Wayne and his studio, Holetown
Thursday, 8 April 2010, 17:30

It's raining now. Unusual for this time of year, people are saying. But it has been raining for four consecutive days—even more unusual. The rain is warm, the kind that we, in Michigan, relish in August when we go outside and play in it.

Wayne comes to drive me to his studio. I walk toward the right side of the car, to get in, before I remember that I am on a European-influenced island and passengers get in on the left. Wayne's car is typically small; the streets are narrow. Horn beeps are courteous reminders of proximity and permission, when waiting at a cross street, to override right-of-way and enter the main street.

His filming studio is a loft above a now-vacant bar, once named First Street Limers. A Heineken sign hangs out front and another offers either a lease or business partnership. We park and ascend an outside stairway to a front-side balcony. Wayne produces a key to a large Master padlock on the door hasp, and we enter.

He apologizes for the dust on the floor and a mis-array of items—playing cards, beer or soda bottles, newspaper comic strips, a few pieces to a jigsaw puzzle—that sit atop what might have once been a bar for serving patrons.

Behind that is the center room where an unmade cot, my bed for the next two nights, has a folded blanket and fresh sheet atop one that has seen better days. There are two bathrooms. The shower is in a separate room. There is mud on the shower floor. "That's part of the movie set, and we wanted it dirty," Wayne says as he turns on the water and uses a flexible shower head to spray away the dirt.

A small counter holds an array of travel-size bottles of shampoo and lotions. Above them is a mirror with a corner missing that might have come from a vanity cabinet. These are also part of the movie set—the bottles intentionally transient and the mirror intentionally broken.

Wayne shows me the room at the rear. "This is where we did most of the filming," he explains, flipping a switch that turns on a single red bulb that hangs from an overhead wire. Under the light is a round café table with a music keyboard, a computer keyboard, a sound mixer, and headphones; a microphone on a stand is nearby.

On the wall are painted large abstract images in blue, yellow, black, and red: human figures, a palm tree (or maybe it's a fish standing on its fin). But most attractive is an eye in stark blue and yellow that measures more than a meter across. A single mattress lies on the floor beneath the eye.

The title of the film is to be *Stranger in Paradise*. The room doesn't look very paradisiacal to me.

The studio in which Wayne was creating his movie.

Wayne hands me the key and leaves. I roam the neighborhood. A Thai restaurant is across the street. Next to that is the Oasis bar with palm trees growing in the entryway. A rib place is next door to Wayne's studio. A tiny beer joint with only a serving area and three tables in an open-air canopy is filled with local patrons. The words "Jesus Saves" mark the lintel of a nearly invisible building between the bar and Wayne's studio. The next street features two more nightspots, three restaurants, an apparel shop, and a hardware store.

After checking menu prices, I head back toward the studio and meet the owner of another restaurant I had missed before. With a cockney accent, he says he came from England for a two-week visit 25 years ago. When I decline his invitation to patronize his restaurant, he changes the subject and directs my attention to the host of egrets sitting in the top half of a tall tree. "They come there to roost every night and create quite a squabble," he says.

That night, I go to sleep to the sound of music from the Oasis, frogs that reside within the palms, and more rain.

Caribbean movies at University of West Indies, Cave Hill
Thursday, 8 April 2010, evening

Wayne picks me up at 07:00 and we drive to the Errol Barro Centre for Creative Imagination at the University of the West Indies, Cave Hill Campus. The first of two movies is already in progress when we take our seats in the second row. The writer/producer is professor Patricia Mohammed who has crafted a series of short films on Caribbean culture. The two shown tonight are *Coolie Pink and Green,* which is about the influence of Indian music and culture in Trinidad, and *The Sign of the Loa,* which is on creativity and energy of African Haitians.

Afterward, Wayne and I drink Heinekens in his studio. He teaches filmmaking and says his primary love is to read and write scripts. He has written several and edited those of other producers, but only recently has he begun to produce his own work. He talks of small-scale innovation. "In Barbados, we make do with what we have. If we don't have it, we make it." And he has little regard for mainstream Hollywood movies. "We can't afford spectacles, so we write good, solid stories," he says.

He describes the plot of *Stranger in Paradise*, which he is in the process of shooting in this studio and on nearby beaches and streets. It involves a young Chinese woman who speaks no English, a Barbadian man who speaks no Chinese, and his adopted son, affected by psychological trauma, who does not speak at all. The three live together under strained conditions. The storyline is fascinating, although I'll not elaborate here out of respect for Wayne's creative work in process.

The conversation switches to world politics. Wayne says he and many Barbadians do not understand the illogic of Americans who castigate men, such as Tiger Woods and Bill Clinton, for sexual indiscretion or, as he says, "just for being men," while condoning government leaders, such as George W. Bush, who create wars that kill thousands.

* * * * *

When compiling this book in 2020, I contacted Wayne via Facebook Messenger. He wrote that sometime after I stayed at his place, he was in a "terrible car accident" that made him unable to walk for about a year. He texted that, while he was healing, "The main actors went back to their respective countries and the child actor grew up." Yet, he hopes to complete the film someday, using a body double for the Chinese actress. In the meantime, he's working on a docudrama concerning the Covid-19 pandemic, titled *Mask of Death*, that he hopes to complete in September 2020.

Saltwater swim and freshwater rinse, Holetown
Friday, 9 April 2010, morning

I awaken at what feels like late morning, and, according to the sun—more than two fists above the horizon—it is. But my watch reads 07:30. How can that be? Then, the light dawns. Barbados is on the eastern fringe of the Eastern Time Zone. My home in Kalamazoo, Michigan, is near the west edge of the same time zone. And there is no daylight savings time on this island. My feeling that I have wasted the morning slips away.

I walk two blocks to the beach. A young man asks if I want to snorkel: $25 US for an hour; I decline.

I wade into the water. It's lovely warm. The first few centimeters of water are shallow, then the bottom quickly falls away and I am in the Caribbean up to my waste. A man in a powerboat trolls toward me until I can touch the fiberglass bow of his vessel. He asks if I want to ski: $30 US for 15 minutes; I decline. He asks if I want to go for a boat ride: $300 US for an hour; I decline. He puts the motor in reverse and backs away from the shore.

I swim, drifting on gentle waves.

A native comes from deep water on a blue paddleboard. He's carrying a spear gun and balancing a white bucket. Ashore, he walks to a makeshift table, fabricated from old plywood, painted, and nailed into the crotch of two palm trees. He upturns his bucket and a dozen or more colorful fish, the size of small trout, tumble out and begin to flop on the table. He picks up a knife and begins to scale away their beauty. "Parrot fish," he says. "Pirate fish?" I attempt to confirm. "Parrot, like the bird." Then I understand.

I go back into the water, swimming, floating, luxuriating in saltwater and salt air.

The travel nurse back in Kalamazoo had given me literature that warns against going barefoot on foreign beaches, so I am wearing rubber-soled aqua sox. My feet encounter submerged rocks, and I am glad that I followed that advice. But, standing ashore again, I am aware that these mesh-net shoes are filled with sand. My feet are beginning to hurt. In the flow and ebb of waves at my feet, a piece of something flip-flops a little too lightly to be a stone; I pick it up. It's coral.

I sit and remove my shoes and see cuts on my soles and toes. From my torn skin, I pick bits of sharp objects. More coral. A brassy teen with a tanned and trimmed body and low-riding swimsuit saunters by. "Why do you wear shoes, old man? It is better to feel the sand between your toes." I suspect that he is right.

Rain begins to fall. A beautiful, warm, misty rain. It feels good, rinsing the saltwater from my skin. I walk slowly back to the studio in pouring rain, deciding that I don't need to take a shower when I get there.

Movie on the beach, Surfer's Point, Inch Marlow, Christ Church Friday, 9 April 2010, evening

It's dark, and Wayne and I are traveling on what seems like at least 100 different roads to travel 40 kilometers across the island. He says he is Trinidadian but lived in Canada for 20 years. He had come to Barbados and explored the island, including driving on every road he could find.

At that time, he and his companion in Canada, a German woman, had planned to move to the tropics. "It was neither Germany nor Trinidad. We didn't know anyone here. So it was a neutral place," he explains. But just as they were about to leave Canada in 1989, the Berlin Wall tumbled, and she chose to live in united Germany rather than paradise. So, he came here alone.

We arrive on Barbados' south beach where he has taken me to see a movie: Johnny Depp in *Dead Man,* a bizarre flick that contraindicates this idyllic setting.

This is the island's windward side, and waves are caressing the rocks in a manner that seems too soft for the amount of wind I feel coming ashore. The 24-foot movie screen is set up outside, and I can't help but think that this combination of beach breeze and early sunset sure beats the dusty inland environs of US drive-in theatres that are now mostly defunct due to artificially legislated daylight savings time.

The temp is in the 70s. Wayne wears a heavy denim jacket and wishes he had brought a blanket to wrap around his body. I'm in short sleeves and would have been comfortable in shorts, but then the daytime high temperature in Michigan was in the 30s when I left there two days earlier, and I am now basking in delicious tropical air.

We dine on fish and salad, cooked in a nearby outdoor kitchen. He has a Heineken and I a Chardonnay, served from a kiosk.

The movie proves to be a little too weird for my taste, so I go for a walk when the DVD begins to jump through a series of images characterized by gigantic bit-mapped pixels until finally freezing in a discombobulated still-frame.

Gazing out at the gentle surf and feeling the warm salt air against my face and arms, I realize I cannot possibly capture the spirit of Barbados in a couple of days—no one can—and I wonder if I will come back here at some future time to try.

Inside the main building, I strike up a conversation with Lisbeth who had earlier taken payment for Wayne's and my dinner and drinks. She is Venezuelan and pronounces her name with a silent h. She has lived in Barbados for 19 years and says she still cannot distinguish between some island dialects. So how much could I learn about a single small island in a lifetime, I wonder.

The answer comes from a roundabout direction as our conversation switches to humanity and spirituality. We agree that, at a level above the Earth plane, all creation shares Divine connection. Maybe that is all I need to know about Barbados and Barbadians.

Yet, I have gained practical information here also. This place, Ocean Spray Apartments, is not an "apartment" in the American sense of that word. It's really a small hotel, with rooms on two levels. Most have a view of the Caribbean Sea, the upper rooms have total privacy, and the rates are very, very reasonable.

So, further exploration is tempting and my desire percolates: to travel these narrow island roads, walk the surf-caressed rocks and coral sands, watch movies on the beach, and talk with locals like Wayne and Lisbeth, even if they are transplanted Barbadians.

David the shore-side necklace vendor, Holetown
Saturday, 10 April 2010, morning

I take my breakfast, a banana and a bottle of orange juice, and carry it to the beach as a gentle rain begins to fall. I spot a bench under a tree and make my way there. But another man arrives first. He takes the seat, and I alight in another, previously unseen, on the other side of the tree.

He asks me if I am alone.

I say yes, and he replies, "Like me."

He asks if I am a professor. "You look like one," he says and seems surprised when I tell him no. "I thought you work at the institute," he adds, then seems more surprised when I don't know of the institute. "It is just down the beach," he says, pointing north. "There. They study water and fish."

And I make a point of walking there later.

I ask his name and he replies, "David."

"David, is that a gold tooth with a diamond in it?"

"Yes." His smile broadens. "I found it on the beach." He points south. "By the shipwreck. I had my dentist put it in."

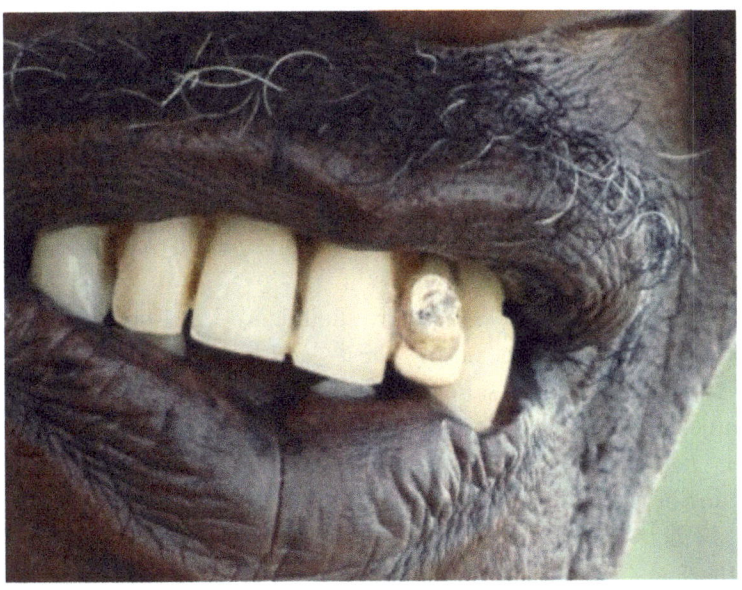

David, the shore-side necklace vendor,
and his diamond-studded gold tooth

He unfolds a colorful towel lying on the sand at his feet, picks up four choker necklaces made of coral, and hands them to me. "Which one you want? $20 Barbados."

One, with a nice balance of white white, dark brown, and tan catches my eye, but I have become accustomed to declining beach offers.

"My children make them. I have more."

My hands are busy with the banana and juice, and I see ants roaming around me on the seat. "Not now."

"If you don't have Barbados dollars, you can buy for $10 U-S."

I finish my banana and cap my juice. Then I move in front of him, squatting in the sand. Most of his wares are longer necklaces for women. He has already shown me the best four for men. My hand reaches toward the one I had admired earlier, and I decide that I want it. A souvenir, I justify, but one I can wear and don't have to dust.

I hand to him 10 Barbadian dollars and 5 US dollars, the equivalent of his initial asking price. I could have haggled, I suppose, but the purchase seems purer this way.

Susie, the bus steward
Saturday, 10 April 2010, 16:15

It's time for me to leave Barbados and head north, then east, across the Atlantic.

Wayne has told me that I can ride either a blue bus or a yellow bus from Holetown to Bridgetown's deep water port. I had ridden a blue bus to Holetown, so I'm glad when the first bus to approach the bus stop is yellow—for variety.

I board with my packs over my shoulders—the 40-pounder on my back and the 20-pounder on my chest—and hand the $1.50 Barbadian fare to a beautiful dark-skinned woman with a rich smile that exudes from deep within her eyes. The woman puts my fare in a worn leather purse that hangs from one shoulder and around her neck, the strap crossing her torso.

She helps me remove my packs, which I set on the floor in front of the first passenger seats. I stand there, too, in the minimal space, close to the feet of two seated passengers. Standing in the aisle on the other side of them, the steward says this bus is privately operated, in competition with the blue municipal busses, and does not have a coin repository; thus, her employment and her purse.

Her English is exquisite, clearly understandable, and her voice is dulcet. But, soon, our conversation is interrupted by many others who board, including five white-skinned persons who are readily recognizable as international travelers. One couple from Cleveland explains they have been exploring the island for the day and are on their way to the harbor, intent on re-boarding their cruise ship by 17:00. The bus steward listens, nods, and smiles from across the aisle. As passengers exit from the rear, this couple moves to fill vacant space.

The two people sitting in the front seats leave, and I sit down. The bus steward sits beside me.

Her name is Susie, and her home is in London. She had returned to Barbados for the passing of her mother a year ago, and is now— "Finally," she says—nearly completed with the family estate work and is ready to return to England. There, she will go back to work as a nurse, but in the meantime, she has enjoyed her temporary role as a Barbadian bus steward. "When you are a sensitive person," she says, "it's good to take time away from caring for others; otherwise, you get burned out."

Trans-Atlantic crossing: Royal Clipper
Embarkation, Port of Bridgetown, Barbados
Saturday, 10 April 2010, 16:30 to 22:00

The sun is shining when I walk a kilometer-and-a-half from the bus stop to the shipping terminal. Three others walk with me, stopping once in a while to take photographs of the blue sea and colorful flowers and trees. A guard at the terminal's entry gate checks my passport while the others show only their vessels' re-boarding pass.

In the terminal, Mariano, the ship's marine biologist and lecturer, is one of two crew members working the onshore check-in desk. He looks at my passport, confirms my reservation, and conveys my cabin number.

Royal Clipper, the world's largest full-rigged sailing ship (photo courtesy of Star Clippers)

A mist is falling as I walk up the gangplank and, unnecessarily but because of habit, request permission to board *Royal Clipper,* the largest of three sailing ships in the Star Clippers fleet of tall ships.

After onboard check-in in the main lounge, a steward shows me to my cabin. My first question is in regard to Internet service, and I learn that, in contrast to previous promises by the booking agency, that service is not working aboard the ship. So, I quickly stow my gear, grab my laptop, and return to the terminal where I had seen a Wi-Fi sign. The mist has added heft and become rain—another consecutive unusually wet day in paradise.

Back in the terminal, Mariano greets me by name without having to check his passenger list. He directs me to a self-help kiosk where I can buy a Wi-Fi card for $5.00 Barbadian, and I am glad that I still have a bill of that denomination in my wallet. For this amount, I can connect to the Internet via my computer for one hour or via a seaport computer for 30 minutes. I need to send a manuscript that I had been editing to my author client, so I choose my computer. But my computer can't locate the Wi-Fi signal.

Back to Mariano. He directs me to the seaport computer. Fortunately, I had made a list of all who I wanted or needed to contact—friends and clients—before departing. However, rather than being able to do so comfortably from my cabin over the next few hours, my location and time was limited to the here and now—fast.

I made a note of the time on the Windows operating system screen and quickly attended to my task. After 28 minutes, I had sent all that I wanted to send, and at 30 minutes, promptly, the computer screen went black. Time ashore is up. Time to go aboard.

By now, the rain has gained even more heft and transformed into a downpour. I bundle my laptop under my anorak and start toward the ship. Fortunately, in the Caribbean, heavy drops of rain do not necessarily equate to a drop in temperature. So, even though soaked, I am warm.

Supper is served at 19:00, and I dine with Jim and Jennie from the UK, Ronald and Marianne from Switzerland, and Bill from Canada. The conversation is international, political, and familial.

At 22:00, passengers gather around the bridge while the crew works the decks. Most are dressed in raingear as mist continues to descend. "1492: Conquest of Paradise," the theme song written by Vangelis for a movie by the same name about Christopher Columbus, plays over loud speakers. Bow thrusters push us away from the dock, and a tugboat helps turn the bow toward the harbor entrance.

The winds are favorable, so the crew hoists the sails. Hearts and spirits rise in unison—at least mine are. We are under way with the dark Atlantic ahead and Barbadian city lights fading off the stern.

We run northwest, parallel to the island coast until we are well clear of the northern end—and probably unseen coral reefs or shoals. Then, we turn northeast, into the wind, and the crew furls the sails. A few passengers remain topsides to watch while the majority descend to the Piano Bar for entertainment by Lazlo, the ship's keyboard artist.

Later that night, visiting the bridge, I learn, with some disappointment, that we will be motoring for nearly 2,000 kilometers until we reach the 30th Parallel where trade winds are expected to be more favorable for actual sailing. So, for the next several days, I experience motor cruising aboard a five-masted tall ship. Oh, well. At least we are at sea.

A view from the sun deck of the bridge deck (foreground), the foredeck, and the bowsprit.

Royal Clipper's three interior decks are shown here: The Piano
Bar and lounge at top, a cabin deck in the center, and the dining
area at the bottom. Next page: One of several beautiful murals.

My first talk at sea
Wednesday, 14 April 2010, morning

I have a microphone in hand and a newly developed PowerPoint presentation at my fingertips. I'm giving a presentation to about 24 fellow passengers. The topic is "Stories: We All Have One. Here's Mine. What's Yours?"

This came about because of an announcement on the daily printed schedule two days ago in which Ximena, the cruise director, extended an invitation for passengers to tell stories, show slides, or otherwise entertain others.

I am reading a poem about my dad and a story about my mom from my first book Cobble Creek, telling about Earth Day founder John McConnell's vision of peace, justice, care of Earth, and describing my brain tumor experience—the subjects of my three commercial books. The audience is attentive; some look enthralled.

I make the offer to sit and talk with anyone who wants to tell me their story or wants free coaching on how to write their story.

Afterward, I receive compliments and further conversation. Two couples who were not in attendance say, "Oh, are you the writer? I wanted to hear you talk but didn't make it there." And so I review highlights with them.

One man confides an emotional event of the previous day, a situation involving his deceased wife of 47 years. He says, "I hadn't planned on telling anyone but when I heard you speak, I decided I wanted to tell you." I listened and thanked him.

Storytelling. It's cathartic, essential, primal.

I am reminded of a conversation over dinner the night before. I said to the people around the table: "If we had a societal meltdown due to manmade or natural disaster that wiped out our communications systems, our highways, our physical and technical infrastructure, who would we turn to first?" Answer: Our local constabulary, medical triage personnel, ministers, mechanics; these are key people who would help us hold ourselves, our emotions, and our machinery together. We would turn to our local farmers and growers for sustenance. And we would rely on teachers, storytellers, artists, and poets to keep our folklore alive. In other words, we would turn to those who, according to current standards of financial compensation, we value and reward the least— and yet are so vital to the full, true human experience.

Mid-Atlantic Neptune ceremony
Wednesday, 14 April 2010, mid-afternoon

I and about 15 others are gathered on the aft deck, dressed in our swimsuits and tied with a faux knot around our wrists. We are led and prodded amidships by the Sports Team: Mariano, the marine biologist, who has painted his face green and is dressed in robes with jangling wads of plastic flotsam tied around his waist; Dave, who is dressed in a black cape, black hat, and fake black beard; Marcus, whose bare face, torso, and legs are striped with red and who carries a crimson trident in his hands; and a young woman with cardboard wings that, due to the breeze, don't want to remain affixed to her shoulders.

The ship is at 24.07.01 N and 49.32.02 W, approximately above the Mid-Atlantic Ridge, a massive submerged mountain range that separates the Eurasian and the North American tectonic plates.

Royal Clipper is heaved to; that is, the sails are unfurled, casting the masts in full canvas regalia, but the vessel is turned and the sails are set in opposing directions so that the good wind is unable to propel the ship one way or another.

"1492: Conquest of Paradise," theme song of the Star Flyer fleet, plays over loud speakers.

Our crime is crossing the ocean's midpoint for the first time. Our punishment is to be determined by Neptune, fabled god of the sea, who sits on the starboard side, dressed in a white robe and adorned with a white flowing beard and white hat. His elevated throne is, normally, a launching platform for a lifeboat. But on this day, it is a dais of justice. Vlad, the captain is nearby, with microphone in hand, to call forth the names of us poor mortals who are now draped by and trapped in a net.

Passengers crossing the Atlantic for the first time are held captive before being found guilty by Neptune. I'm the bearded one left of center.

Ximena, the cruise director, calls the first name. Bill emerges from under the net and is prodded forward to meet his demise.

Neptune announces that his crime will be forgiven if he pays proper homage to the sea: to kiss the fish that Ximena holds before him, to allow her to pour champagne atop his head, and to stand quietly as the other captors cover him with a cracked egg, hollandaise-coated pasta, and flour. Naturally, Bill obeys. Then, he is commanded to jump into a pool of water (one of *Royal Clipper*'s three swimming pools) to rinse the grime from his body and the crime from his soul.

One by one, the captain calls each of our names. Each makes the journey before Neptune and faces Ximena and the fish. We stand before Mariano, Dave, and Marcus with their large bowls of eggs, pasta, and flour. Then, we plunge into the pool. Brrr! It's cold ocean water.

We are laughing, of course, as are the many other passengers who have faced similar judgment on a previous crossing.

Neptune, the god of the sea (right), reads the charges against us first-time crossers while the captain and the cruise director look on.

I prepare to kiss a fish, held by Mariano, the ship's marine biologist and a member of the Sports Team.

Ximena, the cruise director and head of the Sports Team, and I share a shoulder hug and a smile; I'm wearing the necklace I purchased from David in Barbados, as described in the previous chapter.

Thai massage
Wednesday, 14 April 2010, 17:00

"Rearranging the landscape," is a term that a sports therapy masseuse had used to describe treatment to increase range of motion and strength when I was recovering from a torn medial meniscus a decade ago. The term comes to mind now as Kird, whose full name is Waranyu Ratpakdee, tugs and contorts my legs and arms into positions that were once natural—when I was a child—but have become limited with years of living and much sitting at a computer desk.

He pokes and prods with his fingers, thumbs, heel of hands, knees, and feet on all parts of my body. Unlike a Swedish massage where I would lie passively under the smooth, soothing strokes of the masseuse, I am rolled and raised—upside down and right side up—like a ship in a storm. Resistance seems natural but is, in reality, futile if not detrimental.

Why am I doing this? Well, before leaving home, Karen, a friend who is a massage therapist, suggested that I get a massage in every country I visit then write an article about that for a massage magazine. Great idea. Relaxation written off as a business expense.

On Friday, the day I departed Barbados, I received a typical Swedish massage in Holetown. Stepping aboard *Royal Clipper*, I promised myself a massage at the mid-point of the Atlantic. The on-ship spa offered the Thai variety, a new experience for me, and I booked one. It seemed like a great follow-up to the Neptune mid-Atlantic ceremony. Right now, with only my head and shoulders touching the mat as Kird, who is standing, raises my feet to the level of his eyes, I am not so sure. Yet, I endure.

After the massage, I lie on the mat while Kird leaves the room. He is grinning, and the word "masochist" floats through my mind. But when I stand up, I see that I am standing taller. I feel lighter, rejuvenated. This is good.

Apartheid
Wednesday, 14 April, 2010, evening meal

Trevor and Margaret and Stephen and Ann are South Africans. The couples didn't know each other before arriving and met by chance in the dining hall a few nights earlier.

Stephen and Ann own two dairy farms and milk 1,900 head of cattle. They are concerned about a political candidate who is telling citizens of South Africa to kill farmers.

Trevor and Margaret are retired from a security business they have now sold to their son. They are concerned about car thieves who use AK-47s to shoot at security helicopters.

All of them want South Africa to be like it was in the 1980s when apartheid prevailed.

Bob from Pennsylvania
Thursday, 15 April 2010, late morning

Bob is a debonair gentleman in his 80s, and I feel compelled to address him as Robert. He says he lives in Pennsylvania, near Philadelphia, and I mention my research about John McConnell in nearby Swarthmore. We further hone his home as being in Media, the same community where I lived with Robin Harper in 2005 while doing my research. I ask him if he knows Robin, and he doesn't. He asks me if I have heard of a certain professor at Swarthmore College, and I haven't.

His elaboration of this fellow, who he admires as a rare gem among the predominant liberals of that Quaker institution, tells me that Bob is politically conservative. He speaks of the need to tell certain other individuals how to think and act in a proper manner. "And what constitutes a proper manner?" I ask. "Well, doing what's right," he answers, as if I should already know that.

Bob says that humans can never reach perfection. I offer that all persons are one with God, who is perfection, and, therefore, perfection and love and grace are natural to all persons. He acquiesces to some degree by agreeing that God is perfect.

I delve into the concept of communion with all, stating that I prefer that over separation and viewing some people or nationalities as "others." I say that I view humanity as one race: the Human Race. And he agrees.

The conversation moves to health, heredity, and genetics. Bob states his belief that genes control the fate of our health. I tell him that authors I've read and whose books I've edited have debunked that theory and believe that our thoughts and our responses to our environment manifest as either dis-ease or well-ness.

Bob believes that babies are naturally greedy, demanding what they want through tears and tantrums. I counter that babies are naturally loving, willing to share with others. I speak of the possible environments into which a child might be born: that of love or that of fear. And Bob is aghast when I state that some people believe parenting begins two years *before* conception when the mother and father begin to build the home (nest) into which the child will be born. But I continue on, mentioning the YouTube video of the expectant mother who is receiving an ultrasound when the angry father bursts in the room and the fetus jumps inside the womb. And Bob becomes fascinated.

I am aware, as the conversation progresses, that Bob and I are now agreeing more than we are disagreeing. We have reached a common ground. We are sharing laughter and sincerity. We are speaking our truths and respecting the truths of each other. This feels good.

We agree that we are blessed in the United States with an oasis of general freedom from debilitating diseases that remain prevalent in other countries, such as malaria in India and yellow fever in South

America. Bob talks about mosquitoes and how to eradicate them: DDT. "Not one human has been harmed and not one bird egg shell has ever been weakened by exposure to DDT," he says, "but when Rachel Carson wrote *Silent Spring* ... " At that point, my mind moves to images of crop duster airplanes spraying DDT on the people of India, where I will be in another three months, and I decide I don't want to respond any further. I excuse myself from the conversation.

The boy from Germany
Thursday, 15 April 2010, noontime meal

Laurenz is nine, the only child on board *Royal Clipper*, and he is quite all right with that situation. I compliment his good behavior. "He knows his friends are all in school," says Mike, his father, whose command of English is quite good.

I continue with my compliments, including that I took photographs of the three of them on the netting at the bowsprit the day before. Addressing Laurenz, I see that his expression becomes puzzled. Mike translates, and the lad smiles.

Laurenz and Regine, his mother, share rich red hair while Mike's is jet black. They are a handsome family, probably in their 30s, the youngest aboard. Mike praises Laurenz's performance in school, and Regine nods and beams in agreement.

"We took an ocean voyage when Laurenz was five," says Mike, "from Europe to New York to the Caribbean. We figured it would be the last time we could do that because he was entering school."

But now, going into the fourth grade, Laurenz is changing schools and the family decided to travel again. Next year, Laurenz and three of his friends will be in a different school, two towns away from their home.

"Laurenz wants to learn English," Mike explains. "He knows how important that is. They don't have an English program at his current school, so we are taking him to the other school." This move is unusual, Mike says, because German schools are intended to serve only their communities.

"But all of the boys and their parents went to the new school principal together. We told him that he had to take all of the boys or none," adds Regine. "The principal said, 'I want those boys.'"

Before we reach this point in the conversation, Laurenz has excused himself from the dining room table. "He is going to study," Mike says.

Doris' sailing journeys
Thursday, 15 April 2010, evening meal

Doris, who lives in Germany, was married for 30-plus years to an Italian whose idea of a vacation was to go to Italy to visit his family. The husband died three years ago, and she has been traveling, nearly nonstop, ever since—including trips to visit his family.

"I started with the faraway places: Australia and New Zealand," she says. "Generally, I go home for three weeks then back to traveling again for a month or more."

She shows me pictures of the sailing vessels she has been on.

- *Trollfjord,* a Norwegian cruise vessel that she describes as "more a hotel than a ship." She adds that the owners of this ship, the Hurtigruten line, started as a small fleet of mail ships. She calls them "swimming post offices before roads provided adequate mail service; they visited every port along the coast, going into fjords, staying in port 20 to 30 minutes, then sailing again."

- *Finnmarken,* another Norwegian mail ship that is now in Australia.

- *Millennium,* which Doris sailed from Australia to New Zealand.

- A small wooden craft that looks like Christopher Columbus' *Nina, Pinta,* and *Santa Maria.* "This was modeled after another ship that had been caught, buried, and preserved in sand in a river. I sailed this in Rostock, Germany. It's a very flat bottom boat, not fit for ocean sailing, but good for coastal trading."

- *Royal Clipper* three times: in Italy, crossing the Atlantic, and in the Caribbean.

- *Fram,* a Norwegian expedition ship, twice: from Hamburg to Iceland and in the Antarctic. She has booked passages again from Great Britain to Norway in May and to Greenland in August.

- *Polar Star,* an icebreaker.

- *Mir,* the famed Russian tall ship, from Hamburg into the North Sea.

Pirates night
Thursday, 15 April 2010, evening

Those who have made the crossing before came prepared with pirate hats, striped shirts, tattered leggings, and scarves. One woman has a fake parrot perched atop a finger of her right hand. I happened to have a gold bandana—that's all. Pablo, my cabin steward, has loaned me a foam saber with an orange-and-green hilt. These, along with my jet black shirt, will have to do.

In the open-air Tropical Bar, Ximena calls for five contestants to play pirate games. Three jump to join in. No one else, not even those dressed for the occasion, move. Ximena calls my name, and I step forward. Then, another man rounds out the five.

The first game is a test of strength: to hold a diving belt with 5 kilograms of weights with one hand at arm's length. The first to falter is out. Ximena counts to three in English, and we raise our arms. The contestant next to me, Uschi, is a woman at least two decades younger than I and strong. Her belt has less weight than that of the rest of us, all men. I look to the right and the left; these guys, Paul, Ronald, and another man I didn't get to know, are all bigger than I, their biceps larger by quite a bit. I will have to rely on breathing and willpower if I am to prevail. Right. Tell that to my quivering arm. But, just as I think I can't hold out a moment longer, Paul drops his arm; he is out. My arm drops immediately afterward, but I am still in the game.

The second contest requires a blindfold, and there is talk of walking the plank. Instead, each of us is handed a string to which a pencil is attached at the opposite end. A narrow-neck wine bottle is stood upright near our feet. Art, a man from the audience who I had not yet met, comes forward to be my partner. My role is to follow his instructions as he tells me to raise the string, move it right or left or forward or back, then lower it. The deck sways beneath our feet. I can feel wind blowing across my neck. This is not a test of skill but a situation of pure luck. When my pencil drops into the wine bottle, I can't feel it enter. But Art tells me to let go of the string, and I do. I listen, blindfolded. Two others are still striving to accomplish the feat. I am the second to have done it. Art pats my back. I have survived to play another round.

The third contest is a race from a chair on one side of the deck, around a chair on the other side of the deck, back to the first chair—

43

with an inflated balloon between our knees. If we drop the balloon or touch it after the race begins, we have to return to the starting chair and begin again. Ximena counts to three in Spanish, and we begin. I start by hopping but don't like the jarring effect, so I waddle forward. The other two contestants, Uschi and Ronald, are ahead of me. But Uschi drops her balloon. Then does Ronald. I am in the lead and round the chair on the other side of the deck as they go back to start over. The balloon feels comfortable between my legs. My confidence grows. I pick up speed and rhythm. I cruise into the finish line, the only contestant to not retreat and begin again. After dropping his balloon three times, Ronald comes in second. Uschi is eliminated.

David, a member of the ship's Sports Team, pours about three centimeters of water into a pair of short cocktail glasses, making sure that each has the same amount. He sets a straw in each glass. Ximena explains that the winner of this contest will be the person who can drink the water in the glass, through the straw, first. Ronald and I turn toward each other. This looks too easy.

David hands the glasses to us. "You can't touch the straw," Ximena instructs. The wind is blowing the straw around in my glass; the first challenge will be to secure it between my lips. Ximena counts to three in German. I suck on the straw; practically no water reaches the top.

"The straws have little holes," Ximena tells the audience, now laughing. "It is a matter of who has the best lungs," she says in her Mexican accent. With that, I realize that I am bent over the glass, so I stand taller, suck harder, and bring a greater volume of water to my mouth.

I draw again and again and again. The level in the glass is going down—slowly. I draw again and again and again. The last few drops remain. I know that Ronald is beside me, but I think not of him and only of the force with which I draw the water upward through the straw.

The last of the water disappears from my glass; it is in my mouth. I swallow. I raise my arm high in front of me and upturn the glass. Not a drop falls out. The crowd applauds. My victory is secure.

Ximena tells me that my prize is either the drink of the day from the Tropical Bar or a *Royal Clipper* keychain. I choose the keychain, a memento of this victory at sea.

With the straw still in my mouth, I strike a victory pose, holding my glass upside down to show that it is, indeed, empty; Ronald, the other final contestant, wearing white, applauds as does Ximena, the cruise director.

Wisdom from Henning and Gini
Friday, 16 April 2010, evening meal

Henning wears a black patch over his right eye: "Karma in this lifetime," he says. A twinkle in his remaining eye and his smile seems to contradict that sentiment; either he is pulling my leg or he has learned his lessons well. Gini glows with the same brilliance she did the evening before as the best-dressed pirate for Pirates Night.

Henning offers burgundy from the bottle he has ordered and, after deciding to order liver instead of fish, I accept.

I thank them for speaking English. Henning says English is America's gift to the world because it is easy to learn and understand. "But that's only American English," he adds, "not formal British English." Then he asks if I can understand Texas English, adding that it is the most challenging of all.

He says the Chinese have a wonderful way with words, and he loves how one word can have several meanings, depending on how it is spoken. He cites, for example, the word for massage, which can also mean something about killing a horse.

45

I tell the joke about the man who enters a psychiatrists office and repeats, "Doc, I'm a teepee, a wigwam," and the doctor's reply, "Relax, you're too tense." Henning seems to be searching for understanding. Gini asks, "Tipi and wigwam are tents, right?" She has gotten that part of the pun, but they don't laugh until I explain that "tense" means to be stressed. My body language helps explain.

Laughing, Henning says, "That's like the German who goes to the train station and orders 'two to Toulouse.'" Then, he says, "Numbers and letters on German military license plates end in the letter 'Y.' We say, 'That marks the end of Germany.' Y is the end of Germany, get it?" I do, and we all laugh.

The waiter serves Gini's meal first, then Henning's, then mine. "He did that properly," Henning notes. "The lady first, then the eldest man, then the youngest." I suggest that he appears to be younger than I, but he counters with being 72, ten years my senior. Gini, with shimmering dark hair, could be younger. This is a second marriage for both.

He is a maritime architect, a builder of boats—and still working as co-owner, along with a Korean, of his own company. They have offices in China and Germany. Gini works with him so they can be together rather than apart when he travels five to eight months of each year.

He started working with naval destroyers many years after the end of World War II when other world governments again allowed Germany to have a fleet of vessels. He has designed inflatables and sports craft as well as diving gear. Both of them dive and serve as aquatic consultants.

And he has traveled the world: China, Japan, India, many parts of the United States. He speaks knowledgeably of Las Vegas, Los Angeles, San Francisco, Chicago, and Lake Michigan. He produced a promotional movie in 1979 that was filmed on the Rogue River in Washington State and the Colorado River when airplanes and helicopters were still allowed to descend within the Grand Canyon's rock walls.

They listen intently as I describe my upcoming journey. Then Henning's wisdom pours forth. "Be a benefit to everyone not just yourself; that is our business mission," he says. "We value both suppliers and customers. All must profit from our experience together."

He tells of others he knows who travel and come home with only complaints of people and customs encountered in other countries. "Compare but don't criticize," he says.

He talks of mirrors. "People speak of reflecting," he says, "but reflecting is passive. It doesn't mean anything."

I state that I am a sponge, that I absorb energy and need to be around people who laugh and live, like these two dinner mates and others I have met on board. Henning and Gini nod in agreement. "Absorb but don't copy," he says.

Then, especially in regard to India, he adds, "You are going to a very special place. But remember your roots; study Tao or Dao but don't give up who you are." I mention planning my trip to arrive home in time to sail in my favorite race of the year, the Anchorage Cup, a simple one-day linear race on Lake Michigan with Dave, the skipper who mentored me nearly 20 years ago, and my wonderful sailing companion, Will. "That's good," Henning compliments. "Roots don't have to be religion. Remember the roots that link you to your friends."

He advises that life and its many journeys are "a chance and a challenge."

And he closes with: "People experience things and can become bitter but it is better to learn lessons. And every now and then, you need someone to say, 'It's time to get together and compliment each other.'"

With that, we toast for the fifth time during the course of this meal, each of us taking the last sip from our glasses. The bottle is empty.

News from the sundeck
Sunday, 18 April 2010, 13:30

We've been sailing now for about eight days.

I say "about" because the days run together, and, without my watch or the computer clock, I don't have a clue as to what day it is. I'd rather not wear the watch, but there are interesting events to participate in while at sea, and I do strive to be on time for them, even amidst this totally relaxed atmosphere.

I say "we've been sailing" because for the first few days out of Barbados, we motored with the sails totally furled as we headed north-northeast with the wind on the nose or slightly to starboard. Then, about three days ago, we reached the 30th Parallel where winds are typically more favorable for the course and direction we wish to go. We are still going north-northeast but the winds are now from the southwest, pushing us. The sails are out—all except the topgallants, which, if unfurled, would put too much strain on the mast.

47

We are at 33.45 N, 34.47 W, southwest of the Azores. The winds are 15 knots, and our speed is a steady 10 to 13, with following seas. The *Royal Clipper* is pitching and rolling, tossed by swells of seven meters. A gauge on the bridge shows that the rudder, set on autopilot, is swinging back and forth 7 to 10 degrees to port and starboard, passing through center once every 10 to 12 seconds—quite a bit of variance but normal under these conditions.

Walking, whether on deck or below, is a full-body exercise. Sometimes, my feet take a few quick steps to play catch-up with my upper body, and sometimes, I am literally walking uphill. At the passenger meeting this morning, Captain Vlad stood like a swaying stalagmite as he addressed his audience. When passing through a doorway with a latched door, it is wise to close it firmly behind to make sure it doesn't swing unattended.

A woman, Joan, who is 93, traveling alone and famed for climbing the ratlines to the crow's nest on her several previous voyages, fell at supper last night and again at lunch today. Last night, her chair swayed out from under her. Fortunately, Manny, one of the food stewards, caught her by the shoulders and eased her to the floor. I was nearby and saw it all. Today, both Manny and I were across the dining room, and there was no one to catch her. Later, I met Joan walking spryly down the staircase; she said she was waiting for the third fall. "Charming things happen in threes," she said with a smile.

Things happen in three," she said with a smile.

The lower yardarm on the aft mast broke at 06:00 this morning; it's now held in place with a sling. The mast is not being used. One of the ship's two riggers, a burly Russian with a soft smile, is aloft, working on it now. An inclinometer would likely show that we are pitching 20 degrees. He wears a harness.

Yesterday, I discovered the steam sauna. Wonderful. This morning, I was among those who walked two kilometers with Ximena, the cruise director. After that, several of us did calisthenics with Marcus of the Sports Team on the Tropical Deck. Then, I spent an hour in the sauna and missed breakfast. That's okay. I've eaten enough on other days. It's fun to be getting in shape at sea. My skin feels great, too, softer and more natural than normal. Is that the salt air or being away from Michigan's dry winter, or both?

Healthcare
Sunday, 18 April 2010, 21:30

"Robert, tell us about healthcare in the United States," asks Jim who lives in Canada.

Four of us have just finished our dessert, and the wait staff is clearing our dishes, so I wait for them to finish. "I'm not an expert," I say, "but I do live in the US so I have that perspective."

"That's what I want," Jim persists.

Paul from the Netherlands and Robin from Great Britain turn their attention in my direction.

"A few days before we sailed," I begin, "the US Congress did pass legislation to provide universal healthcare. The bill is 1,200 pages long, which is ridiculous. No congressman is going to read that."

"No one can," Jim interjects.

I tell them that the debate is not really about healthcare, even though that is the name used to discuss the legislation. The real issue is what entity is going to provide insurance for healthcare: the government or health insurance companies.

"The crux of the situation," I say, "is the inequity between laws that Congress passes for itself and laws that Congress passes for the populace. Congressional representatives have universal healthcare, yet a large minority voted against the legislation that would allow the populace to have that same privilege. That's why there is an amendment circulating that would require Congress to pass no laws that apply to Congress that do not apply to the populace and no laws that apply to the populace that do not apply to Congress."

"That sounds fair," Robin says with his Liverpudlian accent.

Jim asks if most Americans want universal healthcare, and I respond that I am likely among a modest majority who favor that. "But," I continue, "I think if the media were not involved, those in favor would be a larger, more significant majority."

"Who's against universal healthcare?" Jim asks, and he begins to nod his head even as I utter the first syllables of my response: "Insurance companies."

"And their lobbyists," Jim adds, completing the thought.

"Right," I say. "The lobbyists and the media are scaring people into thinking they won't be able to choose their doctor."

"That's what the media told us in The Netherlands," Paul says, "but after about three weeks, people saw that that wasn't true, and that whole argument went away."

I continue, "The pharmaceutical industry and the health insurance industry are the greatest profit makers in the US, and, I think, greed is a major factor in this debate. I am self-employed and pay my own insurance. My premiums and my deductible have gone up disproportionately to the cost of living over the last five years so that I am getting considerably less coverage for no significant reduction in premiums."

After a few more questions and details, I state, "To me, the irony is that the healthcare debate is more about toeing the party line than it is about healthcare. Our nation is divided by a two-party system. I think that if the Republican Party had proposed universal healthcare, then Republicans would have voted for it and Democrats would have voted against it rather than the other way around."

Jim describes healthcare in Canada, which is government supported. He says that, yes, he does have to wait for treatment to some extent but he much prefers the Canadian way over what has been the US way.

Paul says that government-sponsored universal healthcare used to be the norm in The Netherlands but, recently, the government gave that role back to insurance companies. One result, he says, is that now the cost of medication in The Netherlands is several times higher than for the same medicine in Germany.

Jim and I note that US citizens also see the same medications selling for far less in Canada than in the States.

Robin mentions working in France where universal healthcare is fiscally broken due to the cost of medications and treatments. In the UK, he says universal healthcare is working all right, but there is some consternation because the government withdraws working cancer medications when doctors determine that a patient isn't likely to live more than another year.

I protest that that doesn't seem right. But Jim interjects, "You have to draw the line somewhere or else the cost of treatment up to the point of death will bankrupt the country." Having a second thought, I recall hearing that the vast majority of a person's total healthcare expense occurs in the last year or few months of life, and I acquiesce to his point of view.

As we ascend from the table, I remind my dinner mates that I am not an expert on this subject but I do have the viewpoint of citizenship. "That's what I wanted," Jim says. "All we have is the media, and your perspective is much more valuable than that."

Afterward, I rest in my cabin and consider the word "healthcare," as it was used in our conversation as well as in social and political discussions around the world. "Healthcare" isn't really the right word; the better term would be "sickness care." That's because the political debates are about whether or not to provide money and benefits to *people who are sick,* not those who are healthy.

In truth, there is little or no government money for programs that help people remain healthy. Such programs on fitness, exercise, nutrition, weight loss, and the like—especially perinatal care for expectant mothers—are all provided by private companies or social service agencies. Those are the true sources for "healthcare" benefits in our world today.

Dolphins
Monday, 19 April 2010, 08:00

Ximena is leading six of us on a fast-pace walk around the ship as part of our daily wake-up, work-out regimen. We are on the foredeck when a crewman yells, "Dolphins." Ximena leads us to the port bow, and that is the end of the walk.

The dolphins, perhaps a dozen of them, are romping in the surf of our bow wake, seemingly pushed by the thrust of water ahead of the ship, a few centimeters to no more than a meter in front of or beside the prow. At first glance, it appears the ship could run over them.

One veers sharply to the left, falling aft 10 to 15 meters, then turns abruptly and races ahead of the ship. Others leap forward about five meters and, in unison, leap above the surface to gulp oxygen.

In seconds, they let the ship catch up to them again, romping in the thrust centimeters below the bow wake's foam. One rolls over, exposing its white underbelly but without diminishing its speed.

"They are so fast, and I can't even see them move their fins," I say to Mariano, the ship's marine biologist.

"That's because they are highly efficient," he responds.

We watch them for, perhaps, ten minutes. Then they are gone. This is a sign that we are getting closer to the Azores.

"We'll see them again," says Mariano.

Out on the safety net in front of the ship's prow and next to the bowsprit is a great place to photograph dolphins and *Royal Clipper*'s shapely figurehead.
The bowsprit is the large yellow beam to my right; it is 14 meters long; the ship's four foresails are furled on top of it; when raised, those sails add to the charm and the majesty from this out-in-front, over-the-water view.

Searching for the boon
Tuesday, 20 April 2010, 18:30

I am out on the safety netting next to the bowsprit, admiring the ship's figurehead, taking in the view of sails at sunset, watching dolphins cavort 10 meters below my feet.

I am in a deck chair, reading *The Art of Pilgrimage* by Phil Cousineau, a gift from a friend, Janice, prior to my departure. This book is divided into seven chapters, which the author describes as "the universal 'round' of the sacred journey ... the common rites of pilgrimage": The Longing, The Call, Departure, The Pilgrim's Way, The Labyrinth, Arrival, and Bringing Back the Boon.

I have long experienced the longing. I have finally answered the call. I am two-thirds of the way across the Atlantic, more than 2,000 nautical miles from Barbados and approaching the Azores. I am beginning to sense that I have departed.

Gazing aloft at full sails and blue sky, feeling the ship rock like a child's cradle, I realize how much guilt, fear, self-intimidation, and self-criticism have defined parts of my life. Yet, I am searching. That is one reason I am here—on this pilgrimage. I seek to bring back a different kind of boon.

Shore excursions and the crow's nest,
The Azores, Sao Miguel Island
Wednesday, 21 April 2010, all day

After 11 days at sea, we are in the Azores, Sao Miguel Island, Ponta Delgada.

The Star Clipper line has arranged an island tour for two buses of passengers—one for those who speak English and one for those who speak German—to the village of Sete Cidades (Seven Cities).

The nearby volcano-formed lake contains water that is blue on one side of a bridge and green on the other side. The reality has to do with the way sunlight hits the water, the tour guide says. But legend tells of two star-crossed lovers, a princess and a poor farmer, whose marriage is forbidden. With her blue eyes, she cries tears of blue to form one side of the lake, and from his green eyes comes the green water on the other side.

After the tour, I walk about three kilometers to find a massage therapist who the tour guide has recommended. Against the odds, I am able to book an appointment for later that afternoon. Perfect.

I find a barbershop, thanks to incomplete directions from a patron of a small eatery who speaks only a little bit of English. The *barberia* is on a small street near the center of town with no significant sign to mark its location. The barber speaks no English, but we both know the reason I'm there. The only real question is how much to cut off, and we communicate that through hand motions.

Then, I hustle back to *Royal Clipper* to climb the mast to the lower crow's nest, about 10 meters above the deck. This endeavor challenges my fear of heights, but there is no time for trepidation—I've got a massage appointment to keep and no way to call the therapist—so I climb into the safety harness and clamber up the ratlines.

Three others are there ahead of me: Robin from Liverpool, Doris from Germany who loves to travel by ship, and 93-year-young Joan. I enjoy the view and snap some photos while Paul, the young man from The Netherlands, joins us. Then Dave, manning the belay line below, says someone has to come down to make room for another, so I volunteer. On the deck that features the Tropical Bar, I grab a bite of food and water from the afternoon buffet then rush to the massage.

After another three kilometer walk, I arrive at exactly the appointed minute. Patricia (pronounced Pah-treece-ee-ah) doesn't speak English. But, as with the barber, we both know the purpose of this appointment. The massage is good, as I had expected, but the massage oil was exceptional: sweet and silky, it warmed under Patricia's hands on my back and legs. Afterward, I asked Sophia, the receptionist, how I can buy a bottle. "We make it ourselves, and we don't sell it," she says. A pity? No, a temporary delight, worth sailing the ocean to attain.

That night, aboard *Royal Clipper,* we are entertained by Group Folclorico Ilha Verda, 25 musicians and dancers from Ponta Delgado, men and women who invite the ship's passengers to get up and dance with them. Many of us do.

Joan (right), at 93, is the oldest passenger onboard
Royal Clipper. Here, she stands on the lower crow's
nest attached to the foremast, 10 meters above the deck
(shown below).

International lunch
Thursday, 22 April 2010, 13:00

"Do people in the United States care what people from other
countries think?" asks Paul from The Netherlands. Robin from the UK,
Doris from Germany, and Jim from Canada turn to hear my answer.

"Yes, people from America who think like us sitting around this table do. People who travel among other common people do. But I think there are those in power and government who do not," I reply.

Robin says that he thinks it would be a shame if President Barack Obama is not re-elected for a second term. The others are quick to agree.

The words and terms that all use to describe former President George W. Bush—bluntly and not very politely—describe him as being intellectually incapable of serving as a nation's leader.

Jim says that the US is "a complicated country," then expresses a desire for neighborly watchfulness because, as he says, "Canada catches whatever the US has got."

The general paradigm among this group is liberal with concern for conservative or fundamental extremists in all countries.

Paul tells of an anti-Muslim candidate for Prime Minister in The Netherlands' upcoming election in June who has said that he would legislate a tax on the head garments of Muslim women. "It's like he has a target on his forehead," Paul criticizes.

Similarly, Robin says that Britain will likely have a hung Parliament after its upcoming election in May because no party has a clear majority, a situation that, he says, will favor conservatives and also help Scotland in its move for independence from the UK.

The conversation switches to the presentations of an onboard lecturer, a war correspondent from New Zealand, who has spoken in recent days about the US military campaigns in Iraq and Afghanistan. Paul repeats the lecturer's comment that it will take many years and much money for the US to disentangle itself from those conflicts.

I offer the opinion of many peace leaders who have stated that the US and the world would be much better off if the Bush Administration would have made a choice for forgiveness and understanding, rather than retaliation, after the attack on the World Trade Center. "If we had responded with humanitarian aid, schools, and hospitals, the cost would have been far less and the reward of understanding would have been much greater," I say.

These words are not yet out of my mouth when Paul, who, at 24, is young enough to be a son to the rest of us at the table, says, "Oh, absolutely," while Doris, Jim, and Robin nod their agreement.

Jim says, "They attacked the World Trade Center to create support for terrorists."

"Who are 'they'?" I ask.

"The insurgents from Afghanistan," he replies.

"Please consider that many people in the US consider the events of September 11, 2001, to be an inside job, done by people within the Bush Administration," I offer.

Jim appears skeptical, but Paul is again quick to respond, citing the perfection with which the Twin Towers imploded within their own footprint. He talks about the lack of evidence that it was a plane that crashed into the Pentagon.

I mention the third building, near the Twin Towers, that was intentionally imploded and supposedly contained highly secret documents from the FBI, the CIA, and world financial institutions.

Robin and Doris are also knowledgeable about this conspiracy theory evidence.

I conclude with my observation that the demise of the World Trade Center was the greatest single attack on US soil and, yet, within weeks, the government had all of the forensic evidence moved off site and melted into steel for a battle ship. Everyone agrees that move was very strange, indeed.

The other point on which we agree is that our diplomatic conversations aboard this vessel are stimulating and profound, signs of how people can interact and learn from each other—if they are willing to do so.

US and German politics
Thursday, 22 April 2010, 19:30

Dinner time discussion with Bernhard, Karrin, and Gisela swings from wine to books to politics and societal norms. They are knowledgeable of US politics, including the history of the 20th century. "Why do you know so much about America?" I ask. "Are you the norm?"

Gisela, who was a child during World War II, answers, "After the war, there were the American zone, the British zone, and other zones in Germany. We were under their control. The Americans gave us aid and care packages, so we were curious about them."

Bern, who was an adult at that time, adds, "Germans are the largest European population to emigrate to the US They went there for opportunity. The relatives who stayed behind were curious about where they were living."

They ask if Americans are open to learning about other countries. "The people I know and associate with are," I say, "but I also know people who only want to protect their piece of land and their nationalism."

Gisela brings up the topic of nostalgia, and Karrin, who is married to Bern and speaks limited English, offers the German word, which sounds similar; she makes a point about nostalgia, but due to her accent, background ship noises, and a loud voice at a nearby table, I don't understand. "Many people want to go back to old ways," Gisela explains. Then, she asks, "To what time would you like to go back?"

"I wish that we could go back to the early 1960s, to before John F. Kennedy was assassinated, and that he would not have been killed. Then, I wish we would have gone forward from there." The three Germans nod their understanding.

Then we begin to discuss US presidents. They know the names of most of them, the political parties to which they belonged, and the years or eras when they governed. I admit, with embarrassment, that I have little knowledge of only a few German leaders since Adolf Hitler. They seem to understand and accept that many Americans have a limited view of the history of other nations. "Your country won the war," Bern says as though that explains everything.

Of current politics, Gisele lists parties that are active in Germany: Social Democrats, Christian Democrats, Free Democrats, The Left, Conservatives, Communists, and Green. "None have a majority, so they make coalitions," she states. Bern notes that, as a result, politics are much more complicated in Germany than in the United States. In both countries, they say, the ruling parties shift from election to election; none have lasting power.

Steering the ship
Friday, 23 April 2010, 10:30

I am steering *Royal Clipper*. The officer on watch, Navigator Paulo from Spain, is on the bridge. He has turned off the autopilot and put the ship's direction into my hands—under the guidance of crewman Tiago from India.

This is, by far, the largest vessel I have ever steered, including stints at the wheel of the tall ships *America*, *Pride of Baltimore II*, and *Highlander Sea* on the Great Lakes. But those double-masted schooners, at about 30 meters from bow to stern, are one-third the length of *Royal Clipper*. You can find those stories and others about sailing in me eBook *Great Lakes Sailing 1990s to 2003*.

This ship's wheel turns effortlessly. Because of servo linkage, there is no direct mechanical connection to the rudder, which means I, holding the wheel, cannot feel that submerged blade slicing through the

Given the opportunity, I will take the helm of any vessel,
including *Royal Clipper*.

water beneath our stern. Lacking that sensation, I rely solely on two instruments, the compass and the rudder angle indicator, which reports the number of degrees the rudder is off-center, and on Tiago's instruction and his occasional touch of the wheel, of course.

I notice that this wheel does not have a Turk's Head knot or any other tactile object on any particular spoke that would indicate when the rudder is in alignment with the vessel's center line. That's because, Tiago tells me, on this ship, having the rudder at dead center doesn't necessarily steer the proper course.

With today's current and winds blowing from starboard, for example, we need to hold the rudder at four degrees to port in order to keep the vessel going straight forward on our desired heading of 205 degrees. At first, the compass spins between 200 and 210 as I adjust the wheel a half turn or more clockwise then counterclockwise. But as I acquire a touch with less wheel movement, I bring our wayward path to a steadier 203 to 207.

This seems acceptable to Tiago, and I wonder how much better the autopilot would do.

With other passengers waiting in line, I admit to being a helm hog and turn the thrill over to Bill from Canada.

When I get a second chance to steer an hour or so later, Tiago tells me to put my hand on a certain spoke at the top of the wheel. He says, "Keep this straight up when you're at 205. Turn it to the right if the compass reads less than 205, and turn it to the left if the compass is more than 205." He explains that this spoke, when vertical, positions the rudder to the proper number of degrees off center to steer our desired course.

Watching only the compass and steering according to Tiago's instructions does simplify the task tremendously. And I am able to keep us within a degree of 205. Tiago says that one degree variance is normal because of the fluidity of conditions in which a ship sails. In rougher conditions, two degrees either direction is acceptable. Any more variance than that is not. So, now I know what the autopilot would do.

I smile. I'm doing well. Tiago's assisting fingertips no longer need to touch the wheel.

This is fun!

European table manners
Friday, 23 April 2010, 19:30

"I have a question," I say to Aase from Germany and Paul from The Netherlands. "In America, I would hold my wine glass like this." I lift my glass so that my thumb, index finger, and middle finger cradle the bowl while the two remaining digits balance the stem. "But I notice that you—"

"Ohhh, nooo," Aase drawls "You hold it like this." Her fingers are touching only the stem, with the bowl about two centimeters above her index finger and thumb.

"Actually, it depends on the wine," interjects Paul. "You can hold a glass of red wine the American way because it is supposed to be warmer, but you always hold a glass of white wine by the stem because it's supposed to be chilled."

"Learning to sit properly at the table, with your back straight, is very important in Europe," adds Aase.

We discuss tableware. Observing others aboard ship, I had begun holding my fork in my left hand and only my knife in my right, per European traditions. But Paul offers a refinement to my technique. He informs me that the fork only faces down when holding food to be cut and that it should always be turned over, so the tines are level, when conveying food to the mouth. Except when eating a salad, in which case, it's okay to hold the fork in the right hand.

"When you are eating, you set the fork and knife down on top of your plate on opposite sides," says Aase, demonstrating her fork on the left and her knife on the right. "When you are finished eating," she continues, "you always put both on the right side so the waiter knows to come and remove your plate."

"I was eating in a restaurant with American friends," says Paul, who is a very mature 24, "and I couldn't believe them. They would sit with their menus open and talk. Then, they complained because the service was slow. I told them the waiter was waiting for them to close their menus."

"Yes, that's the signal that you are ready to order," adds Aase.

Sleeping topsides
Saturday, 24 April 2010, before daybreak

The time is 04:00 and I am awakened by deckhands swabbing the deck.

With Captain Vlad's permission, I have been sleeping on the sundeck, a location obviously named for daytime, and not nighttime, use. I had laid out a foam exercise pad and my sleeping bag prior to midnight while the moon was high, its light diffused by a thin veil of hazy cloud. Still awake then, I watched this celestial body seemingly sashay across the sky as, in reality, the *Royal Clipper*'s yardarms, perched between my eyes and the moon, were responding to the pitch and roll of moderate waves off the starboard bow.

The moon is now gone beyond either denser clouds or the horizon, probably the latter, as I hear the sound of water being sprayed from high-pressure nozzles nearby. Fortunately, the swabbies have noticed me. The teak is soaked ahead, astern, and on the port side directly opposite my location. They are working around me—thank you. But rather than sleep in their way, I crawl out of my cozy mummy bag, don my clothing, and stuff my bag in my daypack, which has also served as my pillow.

I re-stow the foam pad and head to the bridge. There, I tell Security Officer Alexander that I have moved and am returning to my cabin. I ask if the crew swabs the deck every morning. He says, "Yes, every morning at oh-five-hundred, but some like to start early."

Lingering topsides, the black night illumined only by a few strands of electric light bulbs on the yardarms and a few security nightlights close to the deck, I relish the peaceful stillness and warm Atlantic air that surrounds me.

Singing in the choir
Saturday, 24 April 2010, 17:30

The impromptu passenger choir consists of eight voices: six men and two women, a rare combination of gender for a singing group. More significantly, we are blending voices from Germany, England, Austria, South Africa, and the US

We've been practicing for four days, about 45 minutes each day. Our repertoire is of the sea, naturally: "Beyond the Sea," "Sailing,"

"What Shall We Do with a Drunken Sailor," "Ode to *Royal Clipper*" (to the tune of "Michael Rowed the Boat Ashore"), and "It's a Long Way to Old Malaga" (to the tune of "It's a Long Way to Tipperary"). The last two contained original lyrics, which several of us altered and I, as the designated writer on board, refined.

Interestingly, all eight singers were first time crossers of the Atlantic, for which we had received a Henley sailing shirt. These became our choir robes.

Royal Clipper's impromptu passenger choir performs before the rest of the passengers.

Disembarkation, Malaga, Spain
Monday, 26 April 2010, 09:30

It's time to get off the ship, literally. The voyage is over.

I'm among the last to disembark, having said goodbye to fellow passengers and new friends at breakfast and while lingering in the Piano Bar and the Tropical Bar.

Stepping ashore in Malaga, Spain, I am in continental Europe—for the first time.

What else can I say?

Reflection: What else can I say?
Monday, 26 April 2010

The people aboard *Royal Clipper* are affluent and knowledgeable of world affairs. They are curious and questioning. Many travel often, either for business or pleasure. Actually, they make no distinction between business and pleasure—all travel is pleasurable. Many have been on *Royal Clipper* or other Star Clipper vessels before—and will do so again.

What else can I say?

The environment and atmosphere aboard *Royal Clipper* stimulates conversation, frequently of an international nature. Yes, there is some general, lighter conversation but nothing trivial.

Most of all, these people have information to share, and they express a desire to interact, explore, and learn from others. I find this to be intellectually and philosophically idyllic.

Does such an experience need to be temporary? What are the parameters and determinants that we need to have in place—as a population or civilization—for this kind of introspection and conversation to occur more frequently if not universally?

Answer: We need an environment of abundance—not necessarily monetary wealth and certainly not greed—but an abundance that comes from having enough and a willingness to share physically and philosophically.

Sometimes, during our conversation, we agreed. Sometimes we didn't. But (just about) always we shared ourselves and our ideas.

What else can I say?

Lots.

What else can I learn?

Lots. If I listen.

The voyage across the Atlantic on *Royal Clipper* was a voyage of saying, listening, and learning.

I wish to carry that over, ashore, into other arenas of my life. I hope it carries over for the other passengers, too. And for you.

So, I ask: What do we do to bring abundance—an attitude of abundance—to the world? I believe it's possible. But how? I invite you to ask yourself that question—then strive to make it happen.

65

Postscript
early in the cruise

To save money, I booked an inside cabin, which means I didn't have a porthole. I figured that if I want to see the sea, I would do so from the deck, not a small round window in my room.

Early in the cruise, I discovered that if I put a towel at the base of my cabin door and a sock over the thermostat, I could sleep in total darkness. How often have I—or anyone—done that? Probably not since the womb. And with the gentle pitch and roll of the ship in its fluid environment, that's exactly where I imagined myself to be.

Aah!

Writing on the sundeck is a good way to affirm one of my
professional mottos: Have Laptop, Will Travel. Yes, I borrowed
this slogan from the television series *Have Gun – Will Travel,*
which appeared on American television stations from 1957 to
1963. Before that, Bob Hope titled his autobiography *Have tux,
will travel,* which was published in 1954.

Malaga, Spain
Unplanned connection
Monday, 26 April 2010, daytime

My computer isn't picking up a Wi-Fi Internet connection at my hotel, Carlos V, so I go in search of a nearby *biblioteca* (library) hotspot to test it there. On my way, roaming through this city's charming streets, I spot a *locaturio* (Internet café). The owner speaks no English and my ears are not ready to comprehend his rapidly spoken Spanish.

A young, tall, thin, dark-complected man interprets for us. The *locaturio* is an option, but I want to have an Internet connection in my room instead of coming out here to check emails. I set off again to the *biblioteca* to test my Wi-Fi settings there.

Within seconds, the young interpreter is at my side. His name is Karim, a 24-year-old Arab Muslim from Morocco who is studying computer science in Malaga. He speaks four languages and offers to fix my computer for a cost of 30 euros. I invite him to come with me to the *biblioteca* and suggest that I will consider paying him some amount of money after we determine the problem and he performs some helpful service. He agrees.

In the *biblioteca,* we have a connection. But Karim shows me that I have two Wi-Fi connection programs on my computer that may be interfering with each other. We return to my hotel to test my computer there. Along the way, he tells me about the historic Arab influence on southern Spain in regard to politics, culture, religion, and architecture.

At the hotel, after some technical manipulation, Karim is able to connect my computer to the Internet—and he shows me how to alter settings for various locations, here as well as elsewhere on my journey. This is valuable information. I pay him 30 euros.

He offers to show me some of the sites of the area, including a nearby Arab fortress, a Phoenician castle, and ancient Roman ruins. I ask if there is a cost for this guide service. He says no; he is happy for the opportunity to speak English, his weakest language. I accept his offer, and we agree to meet later that day at 17:00.

Romano Teatro y Alcazaba
Monday, 26 April 2010, 17:00 to midnight

I eat my evening meal in the café across the road from my hotel, finishing a few minutes before 17:00. At a quarter after, Karim has not arrived, and I am thinking that he won't show when he suddenly appears. I buy him a Coca-Cola, and we set off to see the historic sites.

Romano Teatro is only a block away to the east. It was built in the 1st century during the reign of Emperor Augustus and was used by the Romans until the 3rd century. Rediscovered in 1951, it is still in a state of archeological excavation and restoration.

Through a wire fence, Karim and I view its massive dimensions: radius of 31 meters, height of 16 meters, orchestra of 15 meters, and three main seating areas made of rock that rise for 15 rows. We look across the open pit from the stage area; a tour group of 60 people, sitting on the three upper rows, look like miniature dolls in the distance.

This is part of the arena of Romano Teatro, which is still being unearthed in Old Malaga, Spain. The small splash of color left of center is a group of about 50 people sitting on three upper rows in the seating area. A wall of Alcazaba is at the top of the photo.

Immediately above towers the lower part of the Alcazaba, a Moorish fortress created in the 8th to 11th centuries, in part, with capitals and column shafts from Romano Teatro. Its name comes from the Arabic *al-gasbah,* which, in Spanish, means "citadel." As we ascend the natural topography of the small mountain on which Alcazaba was built, we see the applicable description of that word: "a fortress that commands a city."

At first, we round a sweeping curve at the fortress' base with a high wall constructed of stone and brick on our left, numerous parked cars on a narrow street to our right, a long incline and numerous towers ahead, and a hint of a peak in the distance.

Part of the long road from the base of Alcazaba to its apex is lined, on the left, with walls of the fortress.

Climbing our first set of steps, we get our initial aerial view of Malaga's palm-lined streets and traffic plaza, the nearby bullring and government buildings, and the harbor about one kilometer to the south.

Stopping part way to the top, Kazim and I stop to take in the view of a bullring (above) and a government building with the harbor in the background (below).

At the top of the steps, the path becomes a flat-stone mosaic. Climbing a grade of seven to ten degrees, we walk and stop to take photographs of the ever-changing scene below and a plethora of flowering plants, orange trees, and cacti growing into the hillside.

From an even higher elevation, we see that same government building and the large gardens and fountains with which it is landscaped.

Finally, we reach the apex more than one-and-a-half hours after leaving Romano Teatro. There, we enter a museum that features a miniature model of Alcazaba, artifacts, and several mannequins outfitted as Spanish warriors from the 17th to the 20th centuries.

This table-top model of Alcazaba, found in the museum at the top of the fortress, measures about one meter by one meter.

Back outside, we walk among gardens and elevated stone runways and turrets with loopholes that would have provided the highest defensive positions.

Then we retrace our steps half way down the mountain, walking on the serpentine pathway that borders Alcazaba's exterior walls.

On the way back down, I gain another perspective of the tortuous path with switchbacks that we had ascended to get from the base to the top.

Half way down, we divert toward an urban park that parallels a major boulevard. A wide pedestrian way is filled with international kiosks, representing the food, beverages, and customs of dozens of nations. A sign describes the locale as "II Festival Intercultural. Malaga *abierta al mundo.*"

All together, we walk and talk for seven hours, until midnight, mixing languages: sometimes English, sometimes Spanish, sometimes some of each. Karim fills in details about the origins of this citadel, its link with his Arabian culture, and the influence of Arabs on this historical nationality known as Andalucía.

Near the end of our walk, we admire the view of lighted Alcazaba on the hill above. Karim leaves me at the door of Carlos V then walks another 30 minutes to his home where he lives with several other Moroccan computer students.

Later that night, I enjoy another view of Alcazaba from a plaza in Old Malaga.

Interestingly, I'm not tired, so I roam the ancient neighborhood, amazed at the number of people still out and the number of eateries and drinkeries still open on this late Monday night.

Among the people working in the wee hours are street washers who use a long water hose, attached to a water truck, and a high pressure nozzle to clean the beautiful marble and stone streets. They do this most nights, starting at midnight.

The patterned streets of Old Malaga are not only charming and varied, they are cleaned each night by municipal workers.

In one establishment, I re-encounter Miguel and Nikita, two kiosk operators from northern Spain who we had met and spoken with an hour or so earlier at II Festival Intercultural. Miguel had noticed my shirt with a sailing logo from the Port Huron Yacht Club and initiated a conversation about sailing across the Atlantic, me aboard *Royal Clipper* and he aboard his racing sloop. In the tavern, about an hour after midnight, we consider ordering food and drink but settle for a photograph when the bartendress makes signs that she wants to close for the night.

Nikita, I, and Miguel huddle for a photo taken by the waitress; with the hour too late for food, we simply enjoy the moment.

A walk through history: Romans to Renaissance
Tuesday, 27 April 2010, evening

Karim meets me promptly at 17:00, ready to fulfill his promise of a mixed historical and cultural experience. In the course of the next four hours: we linger in the interior of the Castle of Gibralfaro, built by the Phoenicians in the 14th century, which stands at the base of Alcazaba; go into the Renaissance Cathedral of Malaga, which features two dozen altars and shrines; view a theater devoted to Cervantes; and stand outside the birth home of Picasso who lived in Malaga until the age of 19. Nearby is a park with a statue of the famous painter and only one block from Hotel Carlos V is a museum devoted to his work.

Castle of Gibralfaro at the base of Alcazaba

Exterior of Renaissance Cathedral of Malaga, which is only about 200 meters from my room at Hotel Carlos V.

A primary nave in the Renaissance Cathedral of Malaga.

One of two dozen "minor side altars" in the Renaissance
Cathedral of Malaga.

Statue of Picasso near the home of his birth in Old Malaga.

Old Malaga street culture
Wednesday, 28 April 2010, early evening

The streets of Old Malaga fascinate me. Each is a work of art. Almost all are too narrow for cars. Some contain rows of parked motorcycles and scooters. One is a taxi stand. And most are filled with people walking, talking, strolling, and dining.

In just a little more than one hour, I am on 33 streets, including Plaza de la Constitution, a major gathering place. I walk past Teatro Romano, Castle Gibralfaro, Alcazaba, the Picasso Museum, the Cathedral of Malaga, other churches, numerous shops and outdoor eateries some of which were closed in the middle of the afternoon, and hundreds of people.

With a decent but unobtrusive telephoto lens and my camera steadied on a monopod, I am able to reach out and capture images of people in this cosmopolitan atmosphere.

I take 400 photos.

A chevron design in a marble pedestrian street.

Geometric shapes set with stone and marble.

A simpler surface design created with white marble and black onyx.

And a more complicated pattern of circles, curves, and arrows.

Outdoor tables intermingle with walkways … and with sidewalk vendors and a myriad of small shops, as shown in the next few photos.

The architecture, color of buildings, and patterns in the walkways depict Spain's continental elegance.

The Plaza de la Constitution and the myriad of people in it are the subject of the photo above and the several below.

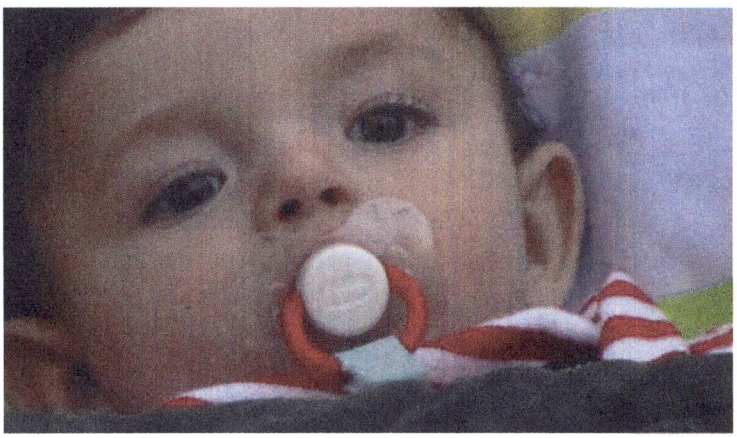

Notice the baby's eyes. I found that, while most adults tend to be distracted by their activities and surroundings, every baby I photographed would lock their eyes on my unobtrusive telephoto lens even if I were many, many meters away from them; it's like they sensed the energy of someone observing them … an energy missed by some adults.

*   *   *   *   *

Tip: When you go to Malaga, stay in Old Malaga; the new part of town is the epitome of beach-front modernity, but Old Malaga is where you will find the rich culture … right outside your door. I also recommend the Carlos V Hotel.

Picasso
Friday, 30 April 2010, morning

The Picasso Museum is alive with visitors of all ages. Several groups of 18 to 20 students who appear to be middle school age are there. The facilitator is animated. Six or eight students' hands are in the air at any time, eager to ask the next question. Teachers stand in the background, sometimes gesturing for the youth to sit on the floor so people behind can see over them. And they do, obediently, courteously.

I roam, as I usually do in a museum, absorbing the overall sensations, stopping occasionally to gather nuance. Picasso's malformed shapes and bacchanalia are engaging, but three quotations from the master, lettered on the walls, speak to me about the journey of adventure and the adventure of life:

> *I want to SAY nude. I don't want to make a nude like a nude. I only want to SAY breast, SAY foot, SAY hand, belly. If I can find a way to SAY it, that's enough.*

> *Love must be proved by facts and not reasons. What one does is what counts and not what one had the intention of doing.*

> (After preliminary text about people who had made magical masks) ... *Painting isn't an aesthetic operation; it's a form of magic designed as a mediator between this strange, hostile world and us ... When I came to that realization, I knew I had found my way.*

Karim's mosque
Friday, 30 April 2010, afternoon

Karim and I are at his mosque for the weekly Friday afternoon ritual. "This is the day I wear my *galabiyya*," he says, his long legs covered in white and his white-shoed feet striding beside me.

Once inside, a man who speaks excellent English greets us warmly but tells me that I cannot go into the inner chamber. Karim had thought I could, but we both accept this decision. "Today is a special service, and it will be full," the man explains. He notes my camera. "Please. No pictures. People come here to pray." I agree, having planned not to take any photos anyway, my practice for reverence during a church service regardless of faith or denomination.

Karim apologizes to me, removes his shoes, and moves into the inner chamber as the man who greeted us provides me with a plastic chair and a suggestion that I place it in the courtyard along a wall on the opposite side from the inner chamber. After a few minutes, he comes back with a closed-network radio and an earpiece. "The service will be translated," he says. "You can listen on this."

I sit back in the chair and lean my head against a window ledge, which tucks nicely under my occipital ridge. I close my eyes and offer my own meditative prayers.

When I hear a loud voice preaching from the inner chamber, I put the earpiece to my ear. The voice from the inner chamber is speaking in Arabic. The translator is speaking Spanish. I don't comprehend the words of either, but I devote one ear to each, wondering if there is such a thing as language osmosis.

Soon, my view through an open doorway to the inner chamber tells me that it is full. Men continue to pour in from the street. Their clothing—white Muslim garb, business suits, casual attire, t-shirts with recognizable brand logos, and athletic shirts that sport the names of American teams—is as varied as their skin color, ranging from mahogany black to extremely pale.

Men already inside the courtyard roll out blue mats. They start on the opposite side of the courtyard from where I am seated, nearest the door to the inner chamber. But within minutes, the last of the mats are rolled close to my chair. Men in Islamic prayer position fill them, too. More men are standing near me, leaning against a wall as they remove their shoes. Even here in the space where I was invited to sit, I am in their extended sacred space.

I pick up my daypack, camera, and water bottle and vacate the chair. By the time I take five steps and look back to make sure I haven't forgotten something, the chair is occupied by a man removing his shoes. He appears to have a handicap and remains seated there while others around him kneel and bow on the blue prayer mats.

I am now in an alcove closer to the main entrance. And that's okay. The speaker has moved to a chant of the Koran and the translator is no longer speaking. I have found another plastic chair and sit in meditative silence, absorbing the spiritual energy of the place and those who are praying here.

Some people I know or have heard speak—those I call a "vocal minority"—promote separation and exclusivity by, ironically, utilizing the inclusive word "all" to drive divisive wedges into the minds of their followers. I have observed that this is true of Americans and Arabians, Christians and Muslims. Their rhetoric, regardless of political or religious belief, falls into the pattern of "*all* who agree with me are superior" and "*all* who disagree with me are wrong, bad, evil, impure."

As Karim and I have walked and talked during three of the last five days, he has told me much about his faith. He has spoken more than I can recall, but the principal spirit of his message is that Muslims are, in general, peace-loving and peace-keeping people. He has stated that there are some who create trouble and want war, and I have said there are militant Christians and Americans, too, some of whom promote war for their personal profit. On these points, we have agreed.

Yet, Karim sometimes exhibits a zeal that prompts me, later while walking from the mosque to his apartment, to ask, "Are you trying to convert me?"

"No," he says, "but if you did, you only have to pray that Allah is the only deity to be worshipped and that Muhammad is His servant."

"I do believe in God," I reply, "but I also believe that each person is already a part of God regardless of which religion he or she practices."

He doesn't reply, and I'm not sure if he agrees with that statement or not.

I sense that his enthusiasm is a characteristic of youth, exhilarated by the opportunity to speak philosophically, in English, with a stranger from the West.

As we talk, he listens to my response, and I hear his voice soften. I feel my body, a bit tense and protective, also soften. That is the beauty of discussion, I realize again for the umpteenth time in my life, while also thinking of times when I had not allowed enough discussion to occur and salve wounds spoken by angry, hurtful words.

Then the majesty of the moment comes floating through my consciousness again. Here is a man 42 years younger than I, walking beside me. He has shown me his mosque, his home, his friends and classmates, his city, his religion, his culture, and his heritage. He has promised to take me to the beach in Malaga later this afternoon and make sure I get to the train station for my trip to Barcelona on time. And I have shown him me, an American Christian, with a different homeland, culture, heritage, and beliefs. He has enriched me during my time in Malaga, and he tells me that I have enriched him, too. Together, we have experienced our commonality.

I and Karim pose outside his mosque.

Barcelona, Spain
Walk of glory
Sunday, 2 May 2010, late afternoon and evening

Majesty. Grandeur. Pomp. Glory. Ceremony. Grace. Fanfare. Gold.

These are the words that stir in my soul as I walk through the site of the 1992 Olympic Games in Barcelona.

The experience has occurred slowly, so I am not overwhelmed by sudden immersion into this arena of elite athleticism. But the feeling of splendor is still strong, and I'm glad that I have come to savor it step by step.

More than two hours earlier, well before sunset, I had looked through a window at the flat of my friends Josep and Chus and seen an intriguing spire directed skyward. I had announced that I would walk there. "It's farther than it seems," Josep had cautioned.

I had eschewed both his advice and a bus, so, instead, I wandered through neighborhoods of high rise, high density population where multiple generations mingle in numerous parks and playgrounds.

Above and below: An urban park and playground in Barcelona is populated by people of all generations.

Discovering a car dealership, I saw an example of Europe's desire and ability to minimize their urban footprint by putting the showroom on the second floor and seven stories of apartments above that.

The Dacia and Renault car dealership on the other side of this
major urban street is totally enclosed on the first and second floor
of this building. The seven upper floors are residences.

At the edge of the Olympic compound, I enter a soccer stadium
where children are kicking a ball. Across the way, in a baseball
stadium, men are playing cricket, their wickets set between second and
third base. From a higher elevation, I look down on tennis courts, track
arenas, and buildings that might be natatoriums or housing. Rising still
higher, I follow a curving road and discover the source of my quest.

This very tall sculpture marks the location of the Olympic Ring
de Montjuic where most of the 1992 Olympic Games were held.

A ramp leads me into the arena where this artistic symbol of Barcelona's modern Olympic Games is based. At the arena's lower elevation, a man and a boy kick a soccer ball in the grass and people run on a dirt track. Yet, there is a hint of a large expanse that stretches into the distance.

Drawn toward the spire, I approach two rows of round columns, about 12 meters tall, and a broad ascending stairway on which a lone individual appears miniaturized.

The step risers are short and the treads deep. These are platforms on which the paramount of the world' athletic youth stood and paraded, displaying nationalistic pride and global glory, in the early 1990s. The steps run perpendicular to gold-lighted fountains.

Water cascades with a peaceful sound over these multiple steps
that stretch for many meters between two sets of stairs that lead
to the Stadi Olimpic de Montjuic Lluis Companys.

Rising above the pinnacle is the Stadi Olimpic de Montjuic Lluis Companys (Olympic Stadium Lluis Companys), a majestic, carved-stone building topped with bronze statues that typify ancient Olympic charioteers. I wonder who or what is Lluis Companys, and Josep later tells me he was a president of the Catalan government in the 1930s and during the Spanish Civil War. The Stadi Olimpic was built in his honor.

The central arch of the Stadi Olimpic de Montjuic Lluis Companys
is topped with larger-than-life bronze statues of Olympic charioteers
(in circle) that look miniscule compared to the building.

From there, I look back at where I have been and the sunset
beyond. There is a temptation amidst such grand dimension to feel
small, like the images of the people in my photographs. But I also feel
the spirit of the athletes who sanctified this place. Their glory is that of
ancient Olympic traditions from which they are descendants, and
triumphant energy lingers from the glory and sound of their presence.

So what I truly feel is, is ... privileged to be here and to have
walked these steps of gold and glory. And gratitude to the City of
Barcelona for keeping this place open and accessible to the public.

The view from the Stadi Olimpic de Montjuic Lluis Companys
stretches for many hundreds of meters; here, I could feel the
grandeur of human accomplishment as well as the smallness of
individual humans, as noted by the people in the photo below.

The business of travel
Monday, 3 May, through Friday, 7 May 2010

The business of travel is time consuming, ever-changing, and sometimes redundant.

I had not booked all of my flight and passage and lodging reservations before leaving home a month ago, so I am completing that task from the road.

I expect to use a credit card for these purchases but am foiled when the booking agent for my passage aboard sail training vessel (STV) *Kaliakra* in the Historic Seas Tall Ships Regatta from Greece to Bulgaria informs me they do not accept that form of payment. Instead, this organization requires that I establish an account with an international monetary exchange, an extra time-consuming step that requires several days of monitoring and emails.

The first complication arises when the monetary exchange company's instructions request a certain bank identification number with a certain quantity of digits. Their instructions use an acronym to describe that number, and I can't find any number with that quantity of digits related to my bank account.

My cell phone isn't working in Europe even though the technician at the local store where I bought it in Kalamazoo said it would. Josep and Chus tell me to use their landline to make international calls, assuring me the cost will be minimal and insisting that I not reimburse them.

I call my cell phone company and learn that the local technician was wrong. My cell phone will not work in Europe because my cell phone company doesn't operate in Europe. End of discussion.

I call my bank and ask about the monetary exchange company's request for the particular account-related number. The banking service person tells me she has never heard of such a number and that maybe it pertains to monetary exchanges between European nations.

I send an email to the monetary exchange company, seeking clarification. After several communiqués, they tell me that their instructions are incorrect and what they want is my bank routing number. Oh, why didn't you say so in the first place? That's easy.

The second complication occurs when the monetary exchange company takes several days to set up my account and process the exchange. Finally, on Friday, the last day of banking business before my departure to Volos, Greece, where I am to board *Kaliakra* and won't have Internet access, the exchange occurs and I receive my electronic ticket. My passage is secure; all is well.

But another complication has occurred when I attempt to pay for an airline ticket with my credit card and learn that my credit card company has blocked usage of the card. I try another card and experience the same result. I again use Josep and Chus' landline to call both credit card companies, which are headquartered in the United States.

The service agents tell me they discontinued service because the cards have been used to make purchases or withdraw cash in Europe. I tell the service agents that I am in Europe and that I have made purchases and have withdrawn cash in the amounts they have on their records. I tell both service agents that I phoned their companies in March, while still in the US, and notified them I would be traveling in Europe, Russia, and India. I ask if my accounts contain a notation to that effect. They do.

I am feeling frustrated with the duplication of effort and feel like saying, "What part of traveling in Europe do you not understand?" But I hold my tongue. One agent tells me her company was simply protecting me. I know this is baloney because the credit card companies are responsible to cover fraudulent use of a lost or stolen card, so they are really protecting their liabilities. But, again, I speak no complaints and, instead, thank them for their diligence and for reactivating my cards.

One benefit of making these calls is that I learn how quickly service agents answer the phone when I dial the collect number for foreign travelers printed on the back of my credit card. There is no long-lasting automated recording, no option buttons to push, no account or zip code numbers to say, no messages telling me how many minutes I have to wait before my call will be answered, no on-hold while-you-wait music. Instead, a real live person answers immediately. I think I'll try calling those numbers from the States when I return.

Through this process, I am grateful for Josep and Chus' hardwire Internet connection over which I feel secure keying account numbers, personal IDs, and passwords. I am also grateful to my cousin and financial advisor Bill who warned me prior to departure, "Don't key your account numbers or passwords into the Internet from a Wi-Fi hotspot. There are people trolling those places searching for such information to access people's accounts."

When discussing these series of events with Josep, he says, "Now you know the difference between being a tourist and a traveler. A tourist goes with all reservations in place. A traveler goes with only a destination from which he might not return."

Gaudi's unfinished cathedral
Wednesday, 5 May 2010, morning

Gaudi's unfinished cathedral.

It is hard to determine which aspect of the Basilica de la Sagrada Familia is more fantastic: the design and craftsmanship or the fact that construction has been going on since 1882, nearly 122 years. At this point in 2010, the project is estimated to be 50 percent complete.

The story begins in 1872 when a Barcelona bookseller by the name of Josep Maria Bocabella visited the Vatican and returned from Italy with the intention of building an elaborate church based on the Basilica della Santa Casa in Loreto, Italy.

Bocabella commissioned the architect Francisco de Paula del Villar who drew up plans for a typical Gothic Revival church. Ground was broken and construction began in March 1882, and the apse was completed by the time Villar resigned from the project one year later in March 1883.

Responsibility for continuance was turned over to architect Antoni Gaudi i Cornet, a proponent of Catalan Modernism, who drastically altered the original plans, making it much, much more ornate. He also slowed the workers' pace, reasoning that "God's work should not be rushed."

When Gaudi died 43 years later, in 1926, the church was estimated to be between 15 and 25 percent complete. For this reason, the church is also known as "Gaudi's unfinished cathedral," even though it is not truly a cathedral.

When I visited the church, I saw construction cranes on the outside, construction scaffolding on the inside—yes, it was permissible to walk inside; many people did—and opulence and grandeur on both the exterior and interior that was truly magnificent … if not gaudy.

With that, I'll let the photos that follow relate the story.

Some of the spires with scaffolding and cranes also in the photo.

A few of many, many smaller individual spires, set at odd angles at the base of the taller spires.

The very tops of the spires are, like the rest of the cathedral, an odd arrangement of shapes, angles, and dimensions.

Above, below, next page: Some of the myriad of smaller, intricate statues and religious scenes that adorn the outer walls of the cathedral.

* * * * *

Postscript: The Basilica de la Sagrada Familia was registered as a UNESCO World Heritage Site in 1984. Pope Benedict XVI consecrated the church on 7 November 2010, six months after I viewed the structure. In 2015, the completion estimate stood at 75 percent; there is talk that it might be completed 2026, one full century after Gaudi's death.

Meanwhile, attitudes have changed significantly over the decades, as has urbanization. Residents of Barcelona are reportedly divided about whether or not to complete the church; potential confusion between it and the city's official Cathedral of the Holy Cross and Saint Eulalia; whether or how much Gaudi's design has been altered since his death. (In 1936, during the Spanish Civil War, revolutionaries set fire to the crypt where Gaudi is entombed, partially destroying his original plans).

Then, there is the fact that ten of Gaudi's 18 planned-for spires are still to be built while the likelihood exists that a nearby tunnel and trains on Spain's high-speed rail system are weakening the church's foundation and stability.

Montserrat
Thursday, 6 May 2010, all day

The name Montserrat means "jagged mountain" in Spanish. The name is derived from the mountain's serrated skyline of pink conglomerate sedimentary rock that is popular with climbers. The mountain is the site of a Benedictine abbey, Santa Maria de Montserrat, and it is accessible from Barcelona via a one-hour ride on a commuter train.

The abbey's huge basilica is filled with people, many of them youth groups, who have come to hear L'Escolania, the famed boys' choir of alto and soprano voices, intone liturgical Latin as part of the twice-daily services.

The abbey at Montserrat is filled with people who come to hear
L'Escolania, the famed boys' choir, who are visible in the
photo on the next page.

Afterward, I light a votive candle to express my gratitude then go in search of a higher sanctuary.

I have already risen a few meters in elevation aboard the train from Barcelona, traveling to the station stop designated for this holy place that attracts over two million tourists and pilgrims each year.

From the station stop, I took the aerial cable car, Aeri de Montserrat, quickly rising above a river and a two-lane highway that snakes at the base of the valley.

The next conveyance will be the Funicular de Sant Joan, a rail tram. Then, I will walk to Sant Jeroni, the highest point on the mountain at an altitude of 1,150 meters.

The guide map says this walk, of about four or five kilometers, will take a little more than an hour. But I soon learn that estimate is optimistic or created by someone younger who may have been running, and I require nearly two hours to make the journey. But that's okay. The place is lovely and quiet, and the walk is relaxing as well as tiring.

The rock formations are families of conical domes that, to me, appear as round gnomes, garbed in antebellum skirts, with flabby arms, bald heads, slitted eyes, and long flowing noses.

Each dome actually consists of what must be trillions of small to cobble-sized composited stones compressed together by Earth's pressures, bound by now-solidified molten liquid, and partially eroded by once-prevalent seas.

From some vantage points, it is possible to look down upon the monastery and basilica complex that also includes souvenir shops, restaurants, and statue-lined meditation trails. Sant Jeroni is said to offer a spectacular 360-degree view of locations far in the distance, but clouds have blown in and the wind is biting by the time I reach the top. Eating a candy bar, I sit in the lee of a waist-high stone pedestal that holds a compass dial. On a clear day, the compass would direct viewers' attention to various locales in the surrounding lowlands. Today, I see nothing but gray beyond the handrail that stands three meters away.

Rested but cold, I start my descent only to encounter sunshine within a few minutes. I look back at the peak to see if a potential view from above would tempt me to return. Seeing only the cloud, I choose warmth and continue downward.

The solitude here is pronounced. Birds and other noise makers are absent. Even the wind below the crest is silent. The eerie feeling is dispelled only be an occasional encounter with others. The few making the journey included one couple, two women together, four women alone, a grandmother with a toddler, and a small group of teens—a number far fewer than the throngs below. All confirm that the estimated trail times on the map are exaggerated.

The view of the valley below Montserrat.

The mountains of Montserrat are populated by stone figures that give the impression of being roundy-doundy humanoids.

After gaining more elevation, I look down at the abbey that is now several hundred meters below.

Cerveza with Chus
Thursday, 6 May 2010, evening

Chus is asking me, in English, if I "want a beer." Because of her accent, I'm not able to understand her; in fact, because Josep has told me that she speaks only Spanish and Catalan, I don't even realize that she's attempting English.

She confers with Josep to see if she is saying the words correctly; he confirms that she is. Finally, I get it. "Oh, *cerveza!*" I exclaim. We laugh. Yes, I know how to order a beer *en Espanol*.

She tells me that *mi Espanol es mas claro* than it was on Saturday, when I arrived. I tell her she is speaking *despacio* (slower), which makes it easier for me *comprendo*.

Even when we don't understand each other, we laugh and smile at our attempts. Overcoming language differences—I won't say "barriers"—is fun.

Oh, and yes, I accept her offer.

A different type of massage
Friday, 7 May 2010, mid-afternoon

I am looking for the massage studio. Josep has given me clear directions. I find the street and the building, but it is a four-story apartment complex. Josep has not provided an apartment number or suite number.

I look at the tenants' mailboxes and security buzzer buttons; no clue there. I ask a teen on the street if this is, indeed, the building I'm seeking; she speaks no English but we are able to confirm that it is. She knows nothing about a massage therapist. She looks up to another teen standing on a third-floor balcony. This teen speaks no English either, but I learn that she knows of no massage therapist in this building. Perplexed, I return to Josep and Chus' flat.

Fortunately, I had been on a scouting mission for an appointment that was still two hours in the future. But Josep and Chus are not at home. I use their landline to call his cell phone; he doesn't answer, so I leave a message. I have no choice but to wait.

He returns my call ten minutes before the appointment time. I tell him of my quandary, and he rings off to call the therapist. He calls me back a few minutes later. Yes, I was at the right building, but the studio doesn't have a name on the mailbox because the building is supposed to be for residential use only, not commercial enterprises. Josep gives me instructions regarding which security buzzer button to press. I return the six blocks to that location just in time for my appointment.

I press the proper button. The door buzzes, and I open it. Inside, I say, *"Ola,"* and a male voice echoes the same word. The therapist is waiting for me on the mezzanine.

He is dressed in a white lab coat comparable to what a doctor in the US would wear. He speaks no English, and I tell him, *"Mi Espanol es piquito."* Or is it *pequeno?* I often confuse those words.

Yet, I quickly ascertain that he is a professional *masaje terapeutico,* licensed *en educacion fisica.* He also practices functional recuperation, chiropractic, and muscular laser therapy. I tell him of my journey and that I am collecting information about massages in various countries for an article that I intend to write. He gives me his card in case I need to contact him later.

He invites me disrobe, leaving my underpants on, and he stays in the room as I do. He directs me to the table, instructing me to lie on my stomach. So far, this is all similar to what I have come to expect from my annual physical examination but not from massage therapists in the US who leave me alone to completely disrobe and then cover myself with a blanket or sheet on the massage table.

His massage is efficient and comforting, albeit with lots of strong tapotement and delivered with more emphasis on recuperative health than complete relaxation. He does not massage my cranium, for example, nor my abdomen.

I ask him if he comprehends the words "medial meniscus," and he says that he does. With faltering Spanish and bits of English, I tell him about the amount of walking I have been doing in the past month, the amount of sitting I have done in years past, my torn medial meniscus of a decade earlier, and the soreness I experienced in my knees while descending the trail from Sant Jeroni at Montserrat the previous day.

He suggests a laser therapy treatment, and I agree, not sure exactly what that will entail—either physically or financially. But he ensures me the procedure *no es entrusivo.*

He palpates the areas around my knees and, using a pen for marking skin, places seven small Xs around each kneecap. I say, "Acupressure points?" and he confirms the accuracy of my guess.

He then turns off the overhead fluorescent light that has been on for the entire previous part of the massage and switches on a soft-glowing desk lamp. Ah, this much more soothing to my eyes.

Then he wheels a machine closer to the table and my lower extremities. He holds a laser point on the designated Xs for 45 seconds each. I feel nothing other than the slight cool touch of the pointer. "Okay, let's see what this is about," I say to myself and relax in the dimmer, more appealing light. When he is finished, he wheels the machine away, turns off the desk lamp, and turns on the fluorescent. He then re-massages the area around my knees.

Using mostly Spanish and a few medical terms common in both his native tongue and mine, I learn that this laser therapy should generate long-term benefit as it rectifies old muscular and ligament maladies. I have the impression that, if I lived in the area, he would recommend ongoing treatment.

It is hard to ascertain any immediate effect from the laser therapy, but over the next few days and even weeks, I feel that my knees are better, stronger. Whether that is due to the treatment or additional strength and tone from extensive walking is impossible to determine. But I do know that I am walking with greater confidence. Is that physical? Or mental? Or both? Is it spiritual?

Nor I am I weakened financially by this service. The total cost is 35 euros (about $45). When I offer a tip, a common practice in the US, he appears offended, so I don't press the point.

Walking with Marina
Friday, 7 May 2010, evening and nighttime

Marina is Russian, an engineer, and speaks beautiful English. She lives in Moscow with her boyfriend who doesn't like to travel, so she goes on her own four to six times a year. She also travels extensively for her work to many parts of Russia. She has come to Barcelona to view architecture, particularly Antoni Gaudi's famed unfinished cathedral. We met on the train from Montserrat the previous day.

During that ride back to Barcelona, I told her I will be visiting Moscow in June, and she offered advice about several hotels along with warnings about the slowness of Moscow trains, the crowdedness of Moscow roadways, and the potential for delay when taking a Moscow taxi. "Leave early for the airport," she insisted.

She also told me that Moscow has two airports, one on the north and one on the south, a valuable piece of information that I, a traveler and not a tourist, didn't know. She said that, judging from the name of the airline I would take from Moscow to Delhi, the airport I want would be Sheremetyevo, the one on the north. When I checked my electronic ticket later that night, I found that she was correct.

I also found an email from her that contained web site links to several hotels in Moscow. I did more Internet research and selected the second of her three top choices.

Heeding her statement that she was bored with walking Barcelona alone and feeling that she had seen enough architecture for one trip, I responded with an email invitation to join me on a walk to the Olympic stadium. Because of that, we are now walking, having met near a plaza that is the roof of a major subway station as the setting sun marks the start of the weekend.

We walk toward then up numerous steps that lead to Palau Nacional (National Palace), which was built for the 1929 World's Fair and renovated for the 1992 Olympic Games. The building is the site of the Museu Nacional d'Art de Catalunya (National Art Museum of Catalonia), a vast collection of Catalan visual art.

As was typical of Malaga, people here in Barcelona are out in throngs, strolling, lounging, talking, laughing, holding hands, and playing games. Marina says this is typical of Moscow, too. I tell her it is not common in US cities except on special occasions, such as festivals, or weekends in places like New York's Central Park; I say that most of the time people in large cities use the sidewalks only to get to work or a store and that people in smaller cities drive. She says she doesn't own a car and that her flat is tiny but she chose it because it is close to her work.

I begin to wonder if I can live without a car when I return to the US, and I calculate the savings in gas and insurance as well as what we Americans consider the inconvenience of not being able to go anywhere any time we want. With such musing, my appreciation for the European rail and mass transit systems grows.

Traveling from Malaga to Barcelona, I had used Spain's high-speed rail system. The trains run about once every hour at speeds of nearly 200 kilometers per hour (125 miles per hour) on rails that are totally smooth. The reclining seats are comfortable enough for sleeping, and the conductors offer a free bottle of water, a toothbrush, toothpaste, and a sleep mask.

Then, when I went to Montserrat, the rail station to that destination was only one block from Josep and Chus' flat. The bus stop for my transportation to the airport, Josep has told me, is even closer than that.

Marina and I discuss the benefits of traveling alone versus with someone. When alone, we determine, it is possible to go where we want when we want without the need for consultation, discussion, and mutual decisions. Traveling with a companion means having someone to talk with, to build memories with, and to notice landmarks and make joint decisions that might prevent becoming lost. We don't attempt to decide which is better.

We make our way to the Olympic stadium, which she had not seen before. She comments on its vastness but doesn't seem to be as impressed with the majesty of the place as I was five nights earlier. Maybe another characteristic of companionship is that each person gathers disparate impressions.

Later, we discover Poble Espanyol, an outdoor architectural museum that features full-size buildings that, collectively, cover 42,000 square meters, an area the size of a neighborhood. The museum contains 117 buildings, streets, and public squares, all reproduced to scale. It is considered an "ideal model" of an all-Spanish village that represents the typical structures of every region in Espana.

We stroll through a courtyard, down narrow stone streets, up and down outdoor stairways, and past restaurants. We note the nuances of one structure from another. Each building has a small placard with a number that, if we had a guidebook, would have directed us to more particulars. Marina, who had come to Barcelona to view architecture, is delighted with this find.

Around midnight, the streets are still filled with people as we descend the steps in front of Palau Nacional and make our way back to the plaza where we met seven hours earlier. There, we part and head for different entrances to the subway system that will take her in one direction to her hotel and me in another direction to Josep and Chus' flat. We shake hands, a sign of friendship and casual acquaintance, a symbol of thanks for an evening much enjoyed.

Josep and Chus' wedding
Saturday, 8 May 2010, afternoon

Josep and Chus' flat is abuzz with excitement on the morning of their wedding. But the excitement is being generated not by the soon-to-be-married couple but by members of her family, five people in all.

The bride and groom have vacated—Chus early yesterday and Josep later last night—for diverse locations, as is the custom in Spain. They will not see each other again until meeting at City Hall, the site of their matrimonial ceremony.

The two men, Javier and Jose, who are married to Chus' cousins and are the official photographers, leave early. The wives, Mari and Patricia, and Javier and Mari's teenage daughter, Paula, and I share a taxi later, arriving at the plaza outside City Hall about 30 minutes before Josep, who gets there before Chus.

We gather in the shade of the ornate antiquated building's north side and wait as another wedding party slowly exits the building. Across the plaza, several dozen citizens are raising their voices and signs and blowing whistles in protest of Spain's economic conditions. "It's the same every day," one of the relatives tells me.

"The same people with the same issue?" I ask.

"No, different people. Different issues. But a demonstration every day; everybody wants to change the government," she replies.

The nearly constant whistle-blowing is particularly loud and annoying, and I hope they will disperse soon.

Once the previous bride and groom and their wedding entourage depart, we enter City Hall, cross a marble-floored interior courtyard with a brilliant gold chandelier overhead, and ascend a long stone stairway with a Gothic-columned hand rail.

Much to my surprise in this government building, the wedding chamber is as beautiful as a church. Its floor consists of a multi-colored tile pattern, while the vaulted ceiling features multiple chandeliers with light bulbs that give the impression of candles. Tapestries of royal gold and red cover the walls. Exceptionally detailed statues, carved in ivory, depict religious figures. Dark wooden pews with hand-carved backrests are available for guests, while the sacristy, where Josep and Chus will sit, houses extremely high-backed wooden seats topped with numerous detailed columnar carvings suitable for a choir or deacons or judges.

The public hall at which the wedding ceremony takes place is decorated to look like a church.

The ceremony is simple and elegant. Josep and Chus appear before a man dressed in a suit topped by a bright red *stole* across one shoulder. He speaks to them with the caring of a clergy and the authority of a magistrate. Informality allows photographers to be in the sanctuary.

Josep and Chus sit in the two chairs between their witnesses and in front of the minister.

Afterward, Josep and Chus descend the steps and emerge into the outdoor plaza as a married couple. The protestors have departed, and the scene is marked by smiles of love and groups who pose for photographs of their individual and now-combined families.

This is apparently the last wedding of the day here, and we linger even while a city employee makes her way among us, sweeping up the red, pink, and white rose petals we have tossed in the direction of the joyous Josep and Chus.

Chus and Josep, as wife and husband, display their constant good humor outside the public building after their wedding.

We then walk several blocks among stone buildings of old Barcelona architecture with overhead arches, people who are enjoying beautiful Saturday weather, and street musicians. We pass through one of the city's largest outdoor plazas where hundreds of people are mingling and a brass and woodwind orchestra is setting up to play a free outdoor concert.

Our destination is the Colon Hotel where we will enjoy a sit-down dinner. Along the way, the two photographers, Javier and Jose, emulate *paparazzi* as they make dozens of photos of the bride and groom from all angles.

After the wedding, the party moves a few blocks from the site of the ceremony to a restaurant for the reception.

Conversation in four languages
Saturday, 8 May 2010, at the wedding reception

Josep's father, who is also named Josep, and two brothers of Josep's mother, Luis and Fernando, and I are engaged in a challenging conversation. Collectively, we speak four languages—Catalan, Spanish, French, and English with a touch of German, I think—but each of us knows only one well plus a few words in one or two others.

Whenever one of us speaks, at least one other person gives the facial expression for not understanding. But another one or two know enough words in the speaker's language to offer a crude translation. Voices overlap as the speaker and interpreters seek agreement, punctuated by *si, oui,* and *yes.*

While the subjects discussed were obviously important at the time, the lingering memory is that of laughter and smiles and accomplishment—key idioms in the universal language of fellowship and celebration.

Moving on from Spain: Should I? Can I? Hesitation, then courage
Saturday, 8 May 2010, nighttime, and Sunday, 9 May 2010, morning

I'm alone at Josep and Chu's home. The bride and groom are gone on their honeymoon. Chus' relatives have returned to their homes. After enjoying so much companionship and laughter for the previous week, the place feels dull and empty. I feel alone. And scared.

I reflect on where I have been and how I have traveled for the previous five weeks. Everything has been arranged, even mostly planned. I had a couch in Wayne's studio in Holetown. I had a cabin aboard *Royal Clipper* and a captain and crew who knew how to get us across the Atlantic. I had a recommendation for the Carlos V in Malaga and friends who took me into their home here in Barcelona.

Yes, I had made some side excursions, but those were easy and generally in the company of others. Oh, and yes, Josep had been particularly gracious when helping me make the necessary reservations for the upcoming legs of my journey.

But, as soon as I would walk out his and Chus' front door, pulling it locked behind me, I would be truly on my own. Can I handle this? Do I want to?

It would be easier to go to the airport and change my flight, to book a seat on a plane for Detroit or Chicago or even Kalamazoo. But do I really want to do that? Really?

In truth, part of me did. It would be easier, I justified. Less risky.

But think of what I would miss. What would I miss? I don't know. I can only imagine.

Do I want to know?

Yes.

So I pull myself together and decide to continue onward. And I make sure that I have everything I need, especially my passport and money, when on Sunday afternoon, I pull the locked door to my friends' home shut behind me.

Which terminal?
Sunday, 9 May 2010, mid-morning

I am at the bus stop where Josep has instructed me to be. I am early, naturally. It is in a highly residential part of Barcelona but no one is there. I wait alone. The bus doesn't come for a long time. Still no other passengers appear. Thoughts of my hesitation from last night do appear; they haunt me. I shoo them away.

Finally, the bus comes. As is my habit, I ask the bus driver if this bus will take me where I want to go. To the Barcelona airport, El Prat. It will.

With faltering English, a woman asks me which terminal I'm going to. I don't know. I didn't know there were multiple terminals. I relate that I am to fly on Air Berlin. She says I need to get off at the second terminal. Others seated nearby agree.

At El Prat, I stay on the bus as many others get off. I ride on and get off at the second terminal. Inside, I learn that this is the wrong terminal; I should have gotten off at the first. It takes more than 30 minutes—waiting for and riding on an intra-airport shuttle bus—to get back to the first terminal. Thank God that I had left Josep and Chus place plenty early.

Privileged service
Sunday, 9 May 2010, 18:00

About 15 to 20 people stand in casually formed lines between me and the Air Berlin check-in counter. But am I in the right place? Again that question looms.

The information screens display only a generic blue-and-white Barcelona Airport logo, so I ask the man behind me if he knows. *Mi pregunta* (my question) is in Spanish. He replies in German. Then we settle into English, which he speaks fluently. He says we are, according to the message on the directional signboard a few meters away, but he admits that he's not sure either.

He asks my reason for being in Barcelona, and I tell about my friends' wedding. He says he came at the request of a friend to watch the Grand Prix race the day before. "But you don't see the race," he says. "You see only 150 meters in either direction. They zoom by and that's it. Next time, I'll stay home and watch it on TV."

He quickly adds that his favorite sport is windsurfing, which he has done in Hawaii. He loves tall ships, having been to regattas in Kiel, a German seaport on the Baltic Sea, and has been on the Russian tall ship *Mir* twice.

He speaks of the current election in Germany in which a coalition of the Communist Party and the Socialist Party won. "Interesting," he says, "that 20 years after the Berlin Wall came down, the Communists have taken control of the German government again."

He tells me that he runs his own business and disagrees with the German government's policy that people who don't work get paid not to work. "They get the same amount whether it comes from an employer or from the government. There's no incentive," he says.

When the check-in monitors come to life and confirm that we are in one of three lines for the flight to Dusseldorf, he mentions that his wife works for Air Berlin. Then, when one of the overhead monitors indicates the line to our left is for privileged passengers, he moves forward in that direction.

In contrast to the long line in front of me, he will be the first in line there. No, the only person. Without thinking, I blurt, "May I join you?" He shrugs and tilts his head in the direction of his quick steps, and I follow.

Standing next to him, I lean my backpack against the side of the counter and hurriedly encase it in the protective nylon shell that keeps shoulder and waist straps from getting caught in airline conveyor belts. From my position close to the floor, I look up. He gives me a knowing nod that I interpret is a signal not to say too much or do anything that would look like I don't belong with him.

When he finishes checking his luggage, he says to the clerk, "My friend is from the United States and this is his first time flying to Germany. Can you help him?" She says yes.

"I'll see you at the gate," he tells me, and is gone. A few minutes later, my bags are checked, I have my boarding pass, and am on my way too. But before I go, I look over at the long lines to my right and take a quick head count. All but two of the people who had been ahead of us are still waiting for service.

Privilege has its rewards. Striking up conversations reaps dividends.

Stephan
Sunday, 9 May 2010, 19:00

When I arrive in the gate area, the man who had helped me back at the check-in counter is seated in one of the institutional airport chairs. I sit beside him and say, "Thank you." He nods nonchalantly, indicating that the favor is universal, and I agree that I would have done the same for him.

He offers his hand, and I shake it. He tells me that his name is Stephan and he has four children, one of whom, age 16, flew to see his girlfriend in Sweden for the weekend.

Stephan is an orthopedic surgeon and chiropractor. "In Germany, you can be both," he says. "That's different than in the United States."

We talk of other different medical practices in the two countries. Mostly, he comments on the greater amount of pressure put on physicians in the US He says he looked into obtaining a license to practice in Hawaii—so he could windsurf there—but decided against it.

In his practice in Dusseldorf, he and the 15 employees in his clinic work a normal business day, seeing customers in the daytime hours with an occasional stint of on-call after-hours. Yet, he also talks of the first seven years of his medical career when "you make your fists in your pockets." He asks, "You have that saying in the United States, don't you?"

I ask him to repeat so that I can better understand his question.

"It means," he says, "when you are angry at your supervisors or something at your work, you ..." He balls his fingers into a fist and shoves them toward his pocket.

"Oh," I say. "We have the phrase 'grin and bear it.'"

"Yes, that's it," he says. "You don't show your anger."

He goes on to explain that the first seven years of a German doctor's career is served in the clinic of an established physician. After seven years, the physician is supposed to write a letter of recommendation, indicating that the new young doctor has completed his internship. "But sometimes the physician doesn't write the letter and you have to work longer," he says. "So, to avoid that, no matter what happens, you make your fist in your pocket."

Travel: It's a bargain

I wish to close with a thought about the cost of travel, based on my experience aboard *Royal Clipper*. First, I knew I was going to Josep and Chus' wedding; no doubt about that. Second, I desired to go by boat, preferably a sailboat.

I checked the cost and duration of a flight: about $700 to $900 dollars one way, arrive on the same day of departure. Cost per day: $700 to $900.

I checked the cost and duration of a cruise line steamship: about $1,500 one way, arrive seven days after departure. Cost per day: $200.

I checked into *Royal Clipper:* $2,500 one way for 16 days at sea. Cost per day: $150 dollars for room and meals and adventure. What a bargain!

Yes, I did have to fly from Michigan to Barbados, but that flight was cheap enough. *Royal Clipper* was still a fantastic bargain ... and a great adventure.

Appreciation and next book in the Journey *... series*

Thank you for reading this book. It is my joy to share these stories with you.

If you wish to review it, please visit my "Robert M. Weir" author page on amazon.com. There, you will find all my books and eBooks.

For links to my author page, my *Journey* ... page, and my blog sign-up contact screen, go to my web site: www.RobertMWeir.com and click on the orange buttons on the right side of any page.

The next book in my *Journey* ... *People, Places, & Ponderings* series is *Greece, Bulgaria, Historical Seas Regatta May & June 2010.*

About the Author

Robert M (Bob) Weir was born in Port Huron, Michigan, USA, on February 22, 1948, and was raised in his family's farm implement business in the nearby village of Emmett.

He graduated from Port Huron Catholic High School in 1966, Port Huron Junior College in 1968, and Western Michigan University in Kalamazoo, Michigan, in 1970 with a Bachelor's Degree in Communication Arts. He has a self-decreed PhD in Life.

Robert's career is in communications. He worked in radio, television, the school yearbook industry, and as a freelance writer and book editor.

He has authored 28 books, contributed to two by other authors, and written over 200 published articles. He has made dozens of presentations, speaking primarily about people, peace, social justice, travel/adventure, and the environment.

As a contract writer for business and industry, he developed and delivered more than two dozen training courses in the realm of management skills and technology.

Robert also served as a consultant and book editor for both established and emerging authors whose topics are primarily in the nonfiction realm of holistic health, metaphysics, human relations, and spirituality.

Reach Robert through his web site: www.RobertMWeir.com.

Made in the USA
Monee, IL
22 February 2023

28436878R00075